"BEFORE THERE WERE TROLLEY DOLLIES"

by

ANGELA WALLER

Pen Press

First published in Great Britain by Pen Press

All paper used in the printing of this book has been made from wood
grown in managed, sustainable forests.

ISBN13: 978-1-906710-96-5

Printed and bound in the UK
Pen Press is an imprint of Indepenpress Publishing Limited
25 Eastern Place
Brighton
BN2 1GJ

A catalogue record of this book is available from
the British Library

Cover design by Jacqueline Abromeit

My thanks to my husband Harry for his constant encouragement, and to "the girls" who flew with me and who have remembered some anecdotes … no names… you know who you are!

Angela Waller

Angela Waller was born in Cheshire, worked as a secretary in London, then became an Air Hostess for six years in the 1950s and 1960s. After returning to secretarial work, she lived and worked in Libya, the U.S.A., and Canada. She met her American husband in Libya and they moved to England in 1992. Angela has written articles for magazines including *Hello!* and *Sussex Life* as well as appearing on TV's *Newsnight*, *Ready To Wear*, and was a champion on *Countdown*. She now lives in West Sussex and is a frequent guest speaker at clubs and societies.

Angela's first novel, *The Snows of Yorkshire*, was published in 2009. It is a family saga spanning six centuries, and tells the story of the Snow family from the 1400s to the 21st century. It can be ordered from bookshops or by going to Angela's website www.angelawaller.co.uk You can also contact Angela through the website.

Contents

Chapter 1   Welcome Aboard!..1

Chapter 2   Ready for Take-off..9

Chapter 3   Larger Aircraft, Red Tails and
                      "The Mile-High Club".......................................21

Chapter 4   From WW1 to Flying Saucers...........................35

Chapter 5   'We regret the delay…' 45

Chapter 6   That's Show Business! 57

Chapter 7   Four-footed Passengers.....................................69

Chapter 8   'I Don't Feel Very Well…' 77

Chapter 9   Food, Drink and Hotels....................................85

Chapter 10   The Rarity… the Unpleasant Passenger...........97

Chapter 11   Whoops!..105

Chapter 12   Accidents *Can* Happen 113

Chapter 13   Go East, Young Woman!.................................119

Chapter 14   That was Then; This is Now............................127

Chapter 1

Welcome Aboard!

Nowadays, if a young woman is referred to as a "trolley dolly" it is said in a rather disparaging way. But in the days before there were "trolley dollies" there were flight attendants... and before that there were stewardesses... and before any of them, there were **air hostesses.**

When I became an air hostess, in 1957, it was considered a very glamorous job and was probably the most sought-after job for a woman at that time. The small airline that I joined said that in one year alone they had had about 5,000 applications for jobs as air hostesses and they took on just four of us! On 20th May 1957, I reported for the first day of training at London's Heathrow Airport, and met two of the other three new air hostesses – Ann Pilkington and Joyce Darbyshire – and Prim Kirk joined a week or two later. In the years since we stopped flying, we have all lived in various parts of the world but three of us (Ann and Joyce and I) still meet occasionally when the airline has a reunion and in between those meetings we keep in touch by email.

The small, independent airline that I joined was called Hunting-Clan; in 1960, it merged with two other small airlines and formed British United Airways. Some time later BUA merged with another airline and became British Caledonian, which was eventually absorbed into British Airways.

Right at the start of our training, we were very excited when we were sent to a tailor in London to be measured for our uniforms. We wore what was then a typical "air hostess" style black hat (the style had been designed specifically to cope with windy airports), with a black jacket and skirt, and a white blouse. We were told that the "rule" for wearing our hats was: Wheels on the ground, hats *on*; wheels off the ground, hats *off*. We also had dresses for "tropical uniform" and these were to be worn whenever we were south of the Mediterranean. While in London, we also went (not so exciting!) to have inoculations for a variety of diseases – cholera, tetanus, typhoid Types A and B, and yellow fever, and we also had a booster for our smallpox vaccination. Details of these inoculations were entered into an International Health Certificate, and we were told that we should carry it at all times. 'Don't ever leave home without your passport and your International Health Certificate!' We were also given anti-malaria pills and told to start taking them straight away and continue to take them regularly, so that we were always prepared to go to areas where the disease was prevalent.

The following training days were spent learning about the types of aircraft on which we would be flying, familiarising ourselves with their safety equipment, and learning what to do in the event of any emergency arising. We learned about the various documents and ship's papers that an aircraft carries and for which we'd be responsible, and the forms to be used to make our "report" at the end of every flight.

We were told that when checking an aircraft before the passengers came on board, we should (obviously) check that the aircraft had been properly cleaned, check that there were safety instruction sheets and "sick bags" in the pockets on the back of each seat, and we should check the lavatories because this is where any potential stowaway might hide. If we found one of the lavatory doors locked, we could open it easily from the outside by putting a coin's edge into a small groove that runs across the lock, and turning it. All aircraft lavatory doors can be opened this way from the outside – a necessary precaution not just because of possible stowaways but because of the more likely event that a passenger might have been taken ill inside, having locked the door when they went in.

Meals for each flight were pre-ordered and loaded in the galley before the passengers came on board, but there were forms for us to use to replenish stocks of drinks and cigarettes while away from base, and to order food for either an onward journey or for the return flight. Because the drinks and cigarettes were all duty-free, we had to check the contents of the bar through outward-bound Customs, the officer would then seal the bar, and it was taken out to the aircraft. We weren't allowed to break the seal and open the bar until we were beyond the English coast and the aircraft was in air space that was outside "the three mile limit". When returning to England from an overseas flight, a Customs officer had to check the contents of the bar against our report, which showed all items sold. Wine was carried in quarter bottles, and spirits were in miniatures. Some people collected these miniatures – they never opened them and never drank the contents – but had a collection of the small bottles.

At the end of an afternoon learning about mixing various drinks, especially some of the more unusual or exotic ones that passengers might ask for, one of the training hostesses said, 'You've all worked very hard… now for your reward. What's your favourite cocktail?' and we each mixed and drank our favourite!

Part of our training had, of course, been about dealing with emergencies and the situations in which we might find ourselves as a result of those emergencies. To learn how to deal with the aftermath of a landing on water (called "ditching"), groups of air hostesses would go to a large indoor swimming pool in London where we would practise getting people into an inflated life raft of the type that was carried on each aircraft. This raft was circular, about 10ft in diameter and large enough to hold 35 adults. It had a "double bubble" inflated ridge all around it – two inflated circles, one on top of the other, so that even if one was punctured on being disgorged from the aircraft, there would still be good floatation. The raft would have been turned over so that it was upside down in the swimming pool, with its flat bottom uppermost, and the "double bubble" inflated ridges stood about 2ft high from the water. In turn, each girl would have to swim up to the raft and somehow manage to heave herself up from the water, reaching over that "double bubble". On the underside of the raft (which, because it was upside down, was now uppermost) there was webbing, and by grabbing a section of that webbing you could drag yourself up on to the raft. After hauling yourself up on to it, you would stand on one edge and by pulling on other sections of the webbing, you could right the life raft and get into it. Once a girl was in the raft, she would lean over the double bubble, and pull people up, one at a time, into the life raft. The first person you pulled up should be someone strong, so that they could help you get all the others on to the raft. Some of the people who were doing this training had to lie helplessly in the water, pretending to be injured or unconscious. It was always stressed that when preparing for a ditching, we must always put on our life jacket. As one of the instructors said, 'Don't think that because you are a good swimmer you don't need that life jacket. I don't care if you are an Olympic swimmer… you might break an arm during the ditching, and need the support of a life jacket.' (In fact, one of our air hostesses *had* swum for Great Britain in the 1956 Olympics, which were held in Melbourne.)

We were also told that, if we ever had to ditch, normally (when is an emergency landing on water *ever* "normal"?) a Viking would float for about two minutes. That, we were told, should be enough time to evacuate all the passengers. We all accepted this statement quite blithely but later I realised that two minutes is a very short time. However, assuming that we did get our passengers out safely during that two minutes we should also try to remove as many of the seat cushions as possible, because they could be used as "floatation devices".

A few weeks later, we had additional training and I was sent on a course that covered survival in the different kinds of places you might find yourself after a crash: in the jungle, in the desert, in the arctic, or on water. Some of the things they taught us have stuck in my memory to this day. When the TV show "I'm A Celebrity, Get Me Out Of Here" has people supposedly "in the jungle" having to eat strange food that they call "bush tucker", it reminds me of what I was taught about all the things that can be eaten to help you survive. We were told that a human body can survive for three weeks without eating any food, but only about three days without water. For that reason we also learned which plants can be chopped open so that you can drink their sap. In the absence of water, the sap would provide sufficient liquid intake to help you survive until rescuers arrived. If we had had to make an emergency landing (or had crashed) on land and we could get back into the aircraft when it was safe to do so, obviously we should bring out all the water we could find, plus blankets and the first-aid kit. An axe is carried on every aircraft and you would use it to pry mirrors off the lavatory walls because these mirrors could be used to flash in the sun and draw attention to your location. Another way to attract the attention of aircraft that may be searching for you would be to retrieve as much of the luggage as possible, together with pillows and blankets, and then lay it all out on land or a beach to spell out S O S.

Some of our training covered medical emergencies that might arise on board and every few months a doctor would come to the airport and lecture groups of us. In fact, normally we needed only to be knowledgeable about first aid because you are never very far (in flying time) from an airport and, if necessary, the captain would radio ahead and ask for a doctor to meet the plane.

At the end of one of the lecture mornings with a doctor, he asked if anybody had any questions. One of the girls put up her hand and asked, 'We've recently had radar cones fitted to the noses of our aircraft and I've been told that they can make you sterile. Is that true?' The doctor looked at her for a moment and then delivered his answer: 'I wouldn't count on it, m'dear.'

Chapter 2

Ready for Take-off

It is difficult to realise how very different everything was in the 1950s from the way things are nowadays. At that time, passengers flying overseas were mostly men who were travelling on business and very few people went abroad for their holidays. For the most part, foreign travel was the preserve of privileged people who could afford it. The introduction of low-cost package holidays in the mid 1950s changed everything and suddenly, because the prices were so low, foreign travel was available to virtually everybody. Almost overnight, family holidays abroad became the norm. Even so, nobody went to Florida or California or any other long-distance destination for their holiday, mostly because of the time it took to get there in those days. In the 1950s, even a flight from London to Majorca took 5 hours and 25 minutes.

In those early days of package holidays, most passengers were flying for the first time and it was a special occasion and treated as such; nobody travelled in jeans or shorts. But coming back from their holiday they all dressed quite differently. Having been in the Mediterranean sun for the first time and acquired a wonderful tan, they wanted to show it off, and the women wore beach dresses with shoestring straps, and the men wore shorts and open-necked shirts with short sleeves. On arrival back in England as they stepped out of the aircraft, there would be a chorus of 'Oh! It's so *cold*!'

The favourite souvenirs to bring back from Mediterranean holidays were locally made large straw shopping bags and huge straw sombreros, which we had great difficulty stowing on the (rather small) overhead racks.

Another illustration of how much things have changed is that when I went home at the end of my third day of training, and told my parents what had happened that day, I added, 'Joyce is going to work on a flight as an extra crew member next Saturday. She's going to Belfast.' My parents were amazed. 'My goodness… working on a flight so soon! Going to Belfast!' Then I added, 'And Ann is going to Paris!' 'Paris!' That astounded them even more. I paused for dramatic effect before going on, 'And *I* am going to Nice!' My parents had travelled abroad a little but my father looked at me with great longing and said, 'Oh! Going to Nice! I'd *love* to see the Mediterranean just once before I die.' Many years later, when I reminded him of what he'd said, I pointed out that by then he and my mother went to Spain and saw the Mediterranean once or twice every year, and also they had stayed with us when we lived in

California and in Texas. So, as well as seeing the Mediterranean, he'd seen the Pacific, and the Gulf of Mexico.

When I started flying, the aircraft that were used to carry passengers were former wartime bombers that had been converted for passenger use. We had twin-engined Vikings, which had been Valletta bombers in the war, and four-engined Yorks. The Vikings carried 32 passengers on flights around Europe, but only 28 passengers on flights all over Africa because the longer distances between places where we could refuel meant that we had to carry less weight. The Yorks (one of ours had been Lord Louis Mountbatten's personal aircraft when he was in command in Southeast Asia during World War II) were used mainly for carrying cargo but occasionally we carried passengers on them. Hunting-Clan had regular, scheduled flights to several places in Europe, and also regular scheduled flights to East, Central and West Africa. In addition, we were often chartered for "special flights" and for the low-cost package holiday flights.

When you fly on holiday nowadays, if you are on a jumbo, there will be anything from 300 to 380 passengers, and at least ten attendants (trolley dollies!) in the cabin, sometimes more. In 1957, we only had one person in the cabin and as we never employed stewards, it meant that the one person was the air hostess. The rest of the crew were all men – two pilots (a captain and a first officer), a radio officer and a flight engineer. Four men and just one girl... that seemed a pretty good ratio to me! We didn't see much of the men on the crew except when we stopped to refuel and have a meal on the ground, although sometimes during the flight they would walk back through the cabin just to stretch their legs and take a few minutes to chat to the passengers. In those days, there was no fear of terrorist attacks and the door to the flight deck (cockpit) was not locked; in fact, sometimes it wasn't even closed.

Another thing that has changed is that nowadays all airport buildings look very much alike. You can fly to Montreal or Miami, Copenhagen or Chicago, and if you only look at the airport buildings, you won't know where you are. In those days, every airport's buildings were different and were usually built in the style of local architecture. Airport buildings in Spain and Majorca had orangey-red crinkle-tiled roofs, and in Switzerland and Austria the airport buildings looked like huge chalets – almost like oversized musical boxes. When I arrived in Nice on that first flight as an extra crew member, the airport was a beautiful sight. The runway was right by the edge of the sea, the Mediterranean really did look as blue as I'd expected it to be, and the snow-capped peaks of the Alpes Maritimes were in the background. The airport buildings were just single storey, surrounded by hedges of honeysuckle and roses, and you could smell the flowers as soon as the aircraft door was opened.

We had flown to Nice on a Viking and very soon after take-off, the air hostess who was in charge told me that the crew always wanted coffee right after take-off. She poured out cups of coffee, put them on a tray and said, 'Here you are… take these up to the crew.' I looked up the aisle towards the cockpit door. The Viking is a very small aircraft by any standards but the cockpit door looked a long way away… a long way to carry that tray with the cups of coffee! Suppose I spilled them? And worse, suppose I spilled them over a passenger? We had been taught to walk and stand with our knees very slightly bent so that our legs would better absorb the shock of any bumps we encountered and, hoping that that advice would work, I set off. An additional "hazard" on the Viking was that the main spar, where the wings joined the fuselage, went right across the aisle. Getting over this meant two steps up and two steps down. I felt a great sense of achievement when I stepped over the spar without spilling those cups of coffee! The walk up the aisle of a Viking never scared me again, even when I was carrying a tray full of drinks for passengers!

We didn't have "trolleys" in those days and we had to carry out all meals two at a time, and clear away in the same fashion, as well as taking drinks orders and carrying them out to just two or three passengers at a time. One air hostess wore a pedometer for a few flights, and to the best of my recollection, she said that we walked approximately four miles on each one-hour flight – for example from London to Amsterdam or Rotterdam or Brussels.

One airport of which I have memories that are not as pretty and attractive as my memories of Nice, is the old Hong Kong airport, which is no longer in use. When coming in to land there, the approach was a long, winding descent over water, getting lower and lower through a narrower and narrower gap, firstly between high hills, and then as we neared the city, between very tall buildings on each side. On the final approach to the runway, the aircraft was literally lower than the highest floors of nearby apartment blocks and very close to them – so close, in fact, that you could actually look into the rooms in the apartments... I'm not exaggerating! In bad weather, making the landing approach was even more frightening.

Just a few days after I had made that training flight to Nice, I was told that the Chief Pilot wanted to see me. The Chief Pilot! That was almost like a summons to approach God! I was scared stiff and thought that I must have done something so bad that they were going to fire me. Surely I couldn't have done anything *that* bad? Surely I wasn't going to lose this dream job almost as soon as I'd started? When I stood before the Chief Pilot (he didn't ask me to sit), he looked at me long and hard, hummed and hawed, looked out of the window, then back at me and finally spoke. 'Angela, do you think you could take out a flight on your own?' I was so relieved that I wasn't going to be fired that I said 'Oh YES' with enormous confidence.

That first flight alone in charge of the cabin was from London to Belfast and the passengers were members of a ship's crew, who were going to join their ship there. They were all seamen from Pakistan and therefore Moslem. As I started to hand out the dinner trays there was a sudden commotion and I had a near riot on my hands! The catering people had put **ham** salad on each dinner tray. Not one of the seamen would touch the tray, not even to hand it back to

14

me, let alone eat the meal… except for the ship's cook who was Chinese and he was very happy to eat more than one dinner! Normally, special diets didn't present a problem; such meals were ordered in advance and delivered direct to the aircraft. Kosher meals came on board in sealed boxes and we were instructed to hand them to the passengers unopened.

Once I was flying regularly, I found that it was almost like going to work at a new job every time I went on duty for a flight, because we didn't fly "as a crew" but each flight would have a different crew. Every time I checked in for a flight and looked at the crew names listed, I might well find that I didn't know any of them. Even so, as Hunting-Clan was a small airline, very soon I knew everybody, so the "new job" feeling passed off quite quickly.

Women's Lib and women's rights were unheard of in the 1950s, and I cannot imagine that nowadays any airline, or any other employer, would be able to impose the terms and conditions that were applied then. I signed a contract of employment that stated that it was "automatic resignation" if an air hostess got married, and also "automatic resignation" on your 30th birthday. During the time that I was flying, this latter rule was amended and after your 30th birthday, the airline allowed you to continue as an air hostess on a year-to-year basis. In other words, each year they would check to see if you still looked "presentable".

I knew one girl who was married and kept it secret, and obviously couldn't wear her wedding ring on her wedding finger, so she wore it on a gold chain around her neck, where it was hidden by her high-necked blouse. But even that contravened rules that were strictly enforced; we were not allowed to wear any jewellery when in uniform, except an engagement ring and small plain gold studs if our ears were pierced. Soon after I had started flying, someone asked me if I wouldn't like to wear a St Christopher medal. 'St Christopher protects travellers,' she said. Yes, that may be so but apart from the fact that it would have contravened the "no jewellery" rule, I don't think the airline would have approved of anything that might indicate that anybody on the crew felt that they needed "protection" while flying!

Everyone thought that as well as being "glamorous", the job was highly paid, but this wasn't true. Before I joined the airline, I had been working as secretary to a vice president of Revlon in their London offices, and earning 12 guineas a week (which translates into £12.60 in today's money). My contract with the airline paid me £5.15.0d a week (which is £5.75). Of course, in addition to our salary, the airline provided our uniforms, except for shoes and handbags. And speaking of shoes, we never changed into flat shoes on board; we wore our high heels all the time.

During our training it was emphasised that we should always take time to talk to the passengers, and not just hand them drinks and meals, and sell duty-free cigarettes. The passengers enjoyed that sort of personal attention and I enjoyed chatting to them because so many people had interesting stories to tell.

One of the air hostesses was very softly spoken and, as it was difficult to hear and understand what she was saying even when you were talking to her on the ground, we always wondered how on earth the passengers or the crew would be able to hear her over the noise of the engines during a flight. One day, when she was working on a Viking and so was the only air hostess on board, she went up front and tapped the captain on the shoulder and said something. 'No, thanks, no more coffee,' he replied. She repeated what she'd said to him. 'No, really, I'm just fine, thanks.' She turned to the first officer and spoke to him. 'No, thanks, no more coffee for me either,' he said. Eventually, after a couple more tries, she managed to make herself heard and told the captain that oil was leaking from the port engine and was spreading over the wing! (The aircraft landed safely at the nearest airport, where the engine fault was repaired.)

We had plenty of opportunity to get to know our passengers on the flights to East, Central and West Africa. These were called our "Safari Flights" and we flew in daylight only, and the crew stayed overnight in a hotel with the passengers. The pace of travelling was much more leisurely at that time, and each leg of the journey took much longer than it does now. On our flights to East and Central Africa we would stay for the first night in Malta and it took the whole day to get there, because we had to stop to refuel at Nice on the way. The more leisurely pace and staying in the same hotel as the passengers each night, meant that we offered a unique service and the passengers felt that they were doing something "different" and "special". Many of our passengers came back year after year to travel with us again.

Because of flying in daylight only and staying overnight all along the route, we took three days to reach Nairobi from London, and four days to reach what was then Salisbury, in Southern Rhodesia – a beautiful city with many of the streets lined with jacaranda trees. Salisbury is now, of course, Harare in Zimbabwe. On our journey to Nairobi, having stayed the first night in Malta, we would then stay for the second night at Wadi Halfa, in the Sudan, and then fly into Nairobi on the third day. Wadi Halfa no longer exists; it disappeared completely under water when the Aswan High Dam was built, and a large area of southern Egypt and northern Sudan was flooded and formed Lake Nasser. On flights to West Africa, just as with the flights to Nairobi, we took three days to reach Accra, Ghana, having stayed the first night in Tangier, the second night at Bathurst in The Gambia, and then arriving in Accra on the third day.

The first place that I spent the night out of England when working on a flight was Malta. During the Nice to Malta sector of the flight, the first officer came back into the cabin and chatted to me. He said that as I was new, he wondered if I'd been to Malta before. I told him I hadn't, so he asked if he could take me out to dinner and then show me some of the sights. I was very flattered and said "yes please" to his invitation. (I discovered later that I should not have been so flattered by his attention. He was what could best be described as "the airline Romeo" and he asked absolutely every air hostess out!) After dinner we walked around

Valletta, the main town on Malta, and as we turned into a narrow street, he said, 'This is the red light district. I'm told that you can get a woman for just a shilling (10p)... and that's for the whole night.' 'What?' I asked. 'Just one shilling for the whole night?' 'Yes,' he said, adding '*and* she'll give you a cup of tea in the morning.' I made what I thought was a quick-witted and funny comment: 'All night *and* a cup of tea... for just a shilling? It can't be very good tea!' The first officer was certainly very good looking, but he was totally lacking in humour and didn't get the point of what I'd said!

Another "first" for me happened when, for the first time, I worked on a flight going south from Entebbe to Nairobi. I was working in the passenger cabin, when the captain buzzed for me to go up to the front. The galley was between the passenger cabin and the flight deck, and I had to pass through it to reach the flight deck to answer the captain's call. However, I didn't get further than the galley because the captain and radio officer were waiting there for me, to celebrate the fact that I was "crossing the line" for the first time. For years there had been a tradition on board ships, that there was a "ceremony" for passengers who were crossing the equator for the first time; the men's faces were lathered and shaved, women had some rather more gentle "washing" of their faces, and then both men and women were dunked in a swimming pool. The captain and radio officer had improvised a "ceremony" for me, which involved washing my face with a rather dirty dishcloth that was in the galley sink. Then the captain presented me with a "certificate of crossing the line" made out on one of the aircraft's documents – signed by "E. Mercer, Captain" with 'King Neptune' added in brackets.

Chapter 3

Larger Aircraft, Red Tails, and "The Mile-High Club"

After I'd been flying for about a year, Hunting-Clan acquired new, larger aircraft. First came Viscounts, and a little later DC6s, and then a few years later, Britannias were added to the fleet. All of these were four-engined planes and carried more passengers than the Vikings or the Yorks. (Although they were larger and carried many more passengers, we still didn't have any "trolleys" for meals and drinks service.)

We had to do some additional training to familiarise ourselves with the new aircraft and the safety equipment on them, the windows that were emergency escape exits, and the best ways of evacuating passengers in an emergency. These larger aircraft had "chutes" which could be deployed if you'd crashed on land and the passengers would slide down them. At that time, almost all women wore skirts, rather than trousers, when travelling and we were told to instruct female passengers to reach through between their legs, grasp the back of the skirt and hold on to it while sliding down the "chute". If you didn't hold on to your skirt, it would ride up and the friction of going down the "chute" would cause rather nasty burns on your bottom and the backs of your upper thighs.

Although, of course, the galley was larger on these bigger aircraft so that we could cater for more passengers, it was still a very cramped space. Even after years of flying and working on aircraft, it was always surprising to me to see just how effectively space was used and how many meals could be stored in the galley. Sometimes when we were flying a longer leg, we would have to carry two entire main meals for all the passengers. When this happened, there was a double "bank" of canisters full of meals on trays, one behind the other. We would serve all the meals from the front canisters as usual, and after they'd been eaten and the trays cleared back to the galley, we would stow the dirty meal trays back in the same canisters. These were then pulled out and pushed to one side, so that we could pull forward the canisters that held all the next meals on trays. The canisters with the dirty, used, meal trays were pushed to the back and the canisters containing the next meals were now put in front of them, ready for use for the next meal service.

Even after we had these new, larger, aircraft, the Vikings were still used for several more years for flights around Europe, and for some charters, and for the low-cost package holidays. But now for all our longer flights we used the

Viscounts and carried 60 or 65 passengers and had two air hostesses in the cabin instead of just one. Also the pattern of our flights changed, and for the journey London to Nairobi or London to Northern or Southern Rhodesia (now Zambia and Zimbabwe) the passengers went straight through to their destination with stops only for refuelling along the route. No more "daylight only" flying; and no more stopping overnight on the way. It was the end of an era when our "Safari" flights stopped; the end of a different and special way of travelling by air. Now, the crews that came from London, southbound, disembarked in Benghazi, Libya, and a new crew went on board to take the flight south. That crew worked as far as Entebbe in Uganda, where another crew would be waiting to take the flight on into Nairobi or Salisbury (Harare). They would spend a day or two in Nairobi or Salisbury, then take the next London-bound flight as far north as Entebbe, where the other crew would be waiting to take the flight on to Benghazi. They would disembark there, and another crew would take over and work the final leg of the flight to London.

Because of "slipping" crews, as it was called, we would work from London to Benghazi, then Benghazi to Entebbe, and then either work a flight into Nairobi and back again, or on to Salisbury, Southern Rhodesia where, after a day or two off, we would set off northbound again. All of this meant that we could be away for 16 or 22 days, but only actually work for 6 or 8 days. Although each working "day" meant that we worked very long hours, nonetheless, it did mean that we had a lot of time off down the route. How different it was from the way things are nowadays, when the "trolley dollies" fly to, say, New York or Miami, and turn around and come home again with almost no time off at the destination city.

The reason for having all those days off down the route was because as a small, independent airline, the government licensed us only to operate two flights each week to Nairobi and one every fortnight to Salisbury. BOAC (as it was then, now British Airways) was the main national flag carrier and had government approval to operate daily flights to Nairobi and Salisbury. So, once we reached Benghazi, we would have a wait of several days before the next southbound Hunting-Clan flight came through.

At that time, Benghazi could be described as a crossroads for many airlines, and just as Hunting-Clan had two whole crews "slipping" there (one southbound and one northbound) at any one time, so did several other airlines. As well as Hunting-Clan, there was another small British airline called Airwork (which was one of the airlines that we joined with later to form British United Airways), and Central African Airways, East African Airways, Air France, Alitalia, and others that all had two crews staying there. On these larger aircraft we had two girls working in the cabin, and there were still four men "up front". It was the same crew ratio of females to males for all the airlines that had crews "slipping" in Benghazi, although some carried one steward and one air hostess, so the high proportion of men to women still prevailed.

24

During the day, we did a lot of swimming and working up a good sun tan (nobody knew about the hazards of too much sun in those days). Several airlines, including Hunting-Clan, had a sailing boat in Benghazi for the use of their crews, and so we did a lot of sailing too. It was mostly the men that sailed but sometimes as they were rigging the boat one would call out 'Angela... would you like to come out with us?' Feeling very flattered to be invited to join them, I'd immediately say 'Yes please,' only to find that once we were out in deep water, one of them would turn round and say 'OK... pop over the side.' 'What?' I'd ask. It turned out that I'd only been invited along because they wanted to practise "man overboard" and needed to have someone willing to jump into the water and just float there, waiting to be "rescued". In the evenings it was party time, every night. Of course, there was (and still is) a firm rule about air crew not drinking alcohol for several hours before going on duty and this was always adhered to very strictly.

During one "slip" in Benghazi, we met a group of men who were there with a British Royal Navy bomb and mine disposal team who were checking the harbour for unexploded bombs and mines that still lay there from World War II. One evening, one of the bomb disposal officers told me that each unexploded bomb or mine had to be given a code name, and that the next one he found would be named "Angela". As we'd all been drinking quite a lot that evening, I didn't think he would remember, but a few days later he told me that an unexploded mine had indeed been code-named "Angela". He had sent a signal to the

Admiralty in London asking for instructions as to how to deal with it, and a signal came back saying: "Tow Angela out to sea and render harmless." I like to think that I'm one of only a few people who have had an unexploded mine named after them!

When we had our time off in Entebbe, mostly we stayed at the Lake Victoria Hotel with occasional trips into Kampala, but sometimes we would go up to one of the nearest game parks. On one occasion, none of the men on the crew wanted to go, so the other girl and I hired a car and drove ourselves up to Murchison Falls Game Reserve, where we stayed for three nights. The main building was a game lodge that had a restaurant, but the "rooms" for sleeping were separate from the main lodge. These "rooms" were actually very large tents, erected on a cement slab, and covered by thatch, and they were scattered around, some distance from the main building. Although there was a wash basin, and jug of water in the "room", the showers and lavatory were a little distance away, along a narrow path. There was a hurricane lamp in each tent and if you went to the lavatory after dark, you took this lamp with you to light your way. Several times, I'd go along to the lavatory/shower area in the morning, and find elephant droppings on the path that I'd walked along when going to the lavatory late the previous night!

At Murchison Falls the mighty River Nile is forced through a very narrow gap in the rocks and forms impressive waterfalls. At the foot of these, where the water was calm again, there were small boats that took tourists along the river. Many different kinds of animals would graze near to the river banks and the boat would cut its motor and drift in quietly so that you could get close to take photographs. Sometimes it seemed a bit *too* close when the "wildlife" you were drifting towards was a 15ft crocodile that had been snoozing on the bank but had woken up as the boat drifted near! The first time I went out in one of these boats I was intrigued to see what appeared to be large rosy-pink blossoms floating in the water. There must have been 20 or 30 of them, and I pointed and asked the boatman, 'What are those?' 'They're hippos' ears,' was the answer! Hippos submerge themselves almost completely in the water, so that only their noses and ears (both of which are pink) are visible. Sometimes it seemed that the boat went dangerously close to these enormous creatures that were floating quietly but we were told that on occasions they would dive under the boat and when they surfaced, they could overturn it. The film "The African Queen" was made in the area around Murchison Falls, and the boat that was used by Humphrey Bogart and Katherine Hepburn was one of the ones that were used for these wildlife sightseeing trips along the river.

Even after we started using the larger aircraft on our African routes, we still stayed overnight with the passengers on our flights to West Africa and it still took us three days to reach Accra. The route had been changed, though, and now we stopped for the first night in Las Palmas, and then the second day we went "around the bulge of West Africa". We called at Freetown in Sierra Leone, and Bathurst in The

Gambia (where we spent the second night), then on to Takoradi, and we arrived in Accra on the third day. We had a day or two free in Accra and the hotel would make up large insulated containers of curry and rice, which we'd take to the beach for lunch. The sea had quite good breakers rolling in, and I learned to surf – the kind of surfing that's done by lying on your stomach on the board and "riding the wave" in. I never ventured to stand up on a surfboard!

On the northbound journey back to London from Accra, when we stopped at Freetown, Sierra Leone, a package was always put on board for carriage to London "in the care of the captain". This package, about the size of a shoe box, supposedly contained uncut diamonds from the large opencast diamond mines in Sierra Leone. I say "supposedly" because sometimes the box was filled with stones and part of the security for the diamonds which, even in their uncut state, would be enormously valuable, was that nobody on the aircraft ever knew whether the box contained "the real thing" or not.

Around the time we changed our flight schedules and the passengers flew straight through overnight to Nairobi and Salisbury, there was a lot of talk about "The Mile High Club" whose members supposedly had sex on board aircraft at an altitude above a mile (5,280ft) high. I never saw any evidence of this happening and I'm sure that if it had happened on *any* of our flights, the story would have gone around very quickly and soon everybody would have heard about it! On overnight flights, once the lights were dimmed and the passengers were settled down to sleep or read, I felt in agreement with Mrs Patrick Campbell who said, in the early 1900s, 'I don't mind where people make love, as long as they don't do it in the streets and frighten the horses.' I didn't care what people did as long as they didn't wake up all the other passengers!

As well as our regular, scheduled flights, we were often chartered by special groups or for special occasions. When the Commonwealth Games had been held in England in the late 1950s, we were chartered to fly the teams from both Northern and Southern Rhodesia home. I was the senior air hostess on the flight and before we left London, I was briefed in the Operations office about the nature of the charter and I was alerted to the fact that the teams had both black and white athletes. 'There may be a problem when you serve meals because some of the white athletes may demand that they should be served first,' the Chief Hostess told me. 'You'll just have to use your initiative to decide what to do and how to do it.' When the time came to serve a meal, not only was there no problem but in fact several of the white athletes insisted on helping us hand out the meals, and they did so in exactly the same order that we always did it – serving the rows furthest from the galley first and then working back, row by row, towards the galley.

Our aircraft were frequently chartered to fly to Perpignan, which was the nearest airport to Lourdes. Passengers were going to the shrine there on pilgrimage, or sometimes hoping for a miraculous cure. I was always filled with admiration for the carers who were travelling with people, often children, who were very ill or were severely disabled. On flights bringing these people home after they'd visited Lourdes, the passengers would all be clutching small souvenirs – religious figures that had been blessed, or bottles of water from the shrine. I never saw or heard of any miraculous cures, but the returning passengers were always filled with joy and thankfulness that they had been able to make the journey. Perhaps those feelings were sufficient to bring them the hope and comfort they sought.

One group of passengers definitely seemed to think that a miraculous event had happened on their flight! A number of African church ministers were flying to London for a major religious conference. None of them had flown before, and all were excited as they boarded the aircraft. They were wearing their long robes and hats, which they did not remove... until … did they think they had witnessed a miracle? A voice from above? The aircraft reached its cruising height and at the same time broke through the clouds into brilliant sunshine. At precisely the moment that the sunshine flooded the cabin, the captain's voice came over the intercom announcing, 'Ladies and gentlemen, we have now reached our cruising altitude of….' The combination of breaking through the clouds, the sudden bright sunshine, and the disembodied, ethereal voice, had the effect of making every single one of the ministers remove their hats!

Without any doubt, the most dramatic event I was ever involved with was when I flew out to what was then the Belgian Congo two days before that country gained its independence from Belgium. Because so many Belgian

30

residents in the Congo feared that there would be a violent anti-Belgian uprising immediately after the independence celebrations, many aircraft had been chartered to fly out all the people who wanted to leave. Our aircraft that was to be used to carry Belgian passengers out of the Congo went first to South Africa carrying freight and only the men on the crew. From there it would go to Elisabethville (another place that no longer exists on the map, having changed its name) ready to take on passengers. I flew out to Elisabethville as a passenger on Sabena (then the Belgian national airline) and spent a day there alone. That day was the one immediately before the official Independence Day, and there was a feeling of tension and anxiety in the air that was almost palpable. Even Belgians who had lived in the Congo for many years, and who had established good friendly relations with business colleagues as well as their house and garden staff, were fearful that violent attacks would be directed at them. Unfortunately, some of their fears were grounded. The day after independence was declared, inter-tribal warfare broke out and there were also attacks on white Belgian residents. We, along with many other chartered aircraft, flew out hundreds of people, some of whom had been attacked and badly injured.

As well as the Belgian passengers on our flight out of the Congo, there was one Englishman. He had been working in the copper mines in the southern part of the Congo and because he, too, had anticipated that there would be problems after independence and that the Congolese currency would be valueless, he had insisted on being paid in gold sovereigns. He offered one of the sovereigns to me in payment for drinks on board the aircraft because it was the only currency he had, but I turned it down and gave him free drinks. How could I take something that was worth (at that time) about £50 in payment for a couple of drinks costing only a few shillings?

During the 1950s and 1960s, at the time that I was flying, many countries in the British Commonwealth gained their independence. It seemed that as soon as the new nation was formed it often changed its name, designed a new flag, and acquired a new national anthem. As well as these three things, most newly formed countries wanted to "show the flag" by having their own airline. These countries didn't go to the expense of buying aircraft, and either training their own crews or hiring them from other countries, but they would contract an airline such as ours to operate an airline in their name. In the case of Sierra Leone, we supplied both the aircraft and the crews, with an air hostess from Sierra Leone on board as an addition to the cabin crew. She would work from Freetown to London, spend the night there, and then work a flight back to Freetown. The aircraft was exactly the same as for our own flights, except that a "sticker" reading "Sierra Leone Airways" would have been applied to the upper part of the fuselage. The sticker was removed once the aircraft was back in England, so that when it went out on service again it was under our own airline name.

BOAC, as the national flag carrier, had more flights to more destinations and with greater frequency than we were allowed. Although relations were always friendly with all other airline crews, and we always got together for parties in the hotels down the route, BOAC crews took every opportunity to remind us that we were definitely "the poor relation". But the time came when we got our own back… and we did so in magnificent fashion. Hunting-Clan was the first airline in the world to paint their tail fins a bright colour. Nowadays, when all airlines have colours and designs painted on their tail fins (some of them downright gaudy) it is difficult to remember that until Hunting-Clan painted their tail fins bright red, all aircraft were either unpainted silvery metal all over or – at most – some airlines painted the upper half of the fuselage white. The only "distinguishing feature" for any airline was that its name was painted along the upper side of the fuselage. When our bright red tails first appeared, there was a lot of joking and wise-cracking, and whenever we passed a BOAC crew in airports, they would sing "Red tails in the sunset" to the tune of an old song with similar words.

However, the time for our revenge came quite quickly! Only about three months after our red tails had first appeared, BOAC painted their tail fins navy blue. All British airlines put the Union Jack flag on their tail but when BOAC put it on their navy tails they found that the dark blue of the Union Jack "bled" into the navy blue on the tails, so they outlined the flag in white. Several of our pilots who were keen sailors and really "knew their flags" were delighted to inform BOAC crews that the Union Jack, outlined in white, is a naval signal that indicates "No pilot on board".

Chapter 4

From WWI to Flying Saucers

As has already been noted, very few people travelled abroad by air for pleasure before the advent of low cost package holidays in the 1950s. Until then, passengers travelled either on business or because it was a very special occasion – perhaps going to visit a relative who had emigrated from England. Sometimes they were emigrating themselves, and in those cases they came on board in a very emotional state, having just said goodbye to family and friends at the airport. Because of the rarity of long distance travel at that time, people who were emigrating knew that there was a possibility – or even a probability – that they wouldn't see any of their friends and relations in England again. I always tried to judge whether it was best to leave them alone with their thoughts and emotions, or to talk to them and make sure they were comfortable. I would keep a careful eye on them and I found that the ones who wanted to talk would catch your eye, and there would be a look that – even though their eyes were tear-filled – made you recognise their need for a short chat.

At that time, quite a lot of people were leaving England for life in Australia or Canada or parts of Africa. Many went by sea and this was the time when the Australian government was subsidising the fares of people who were emigrating there. From Britain the subsidised fare was only £10 and those people became known in Australia as "Ten Pound Poms". Quite often we were chartered to take a plane load of emigrants to different parts of the British Commonwealth, and two or three times I was on flights taking young men to join the police in what was then Southern Rhodesia (now Zimbabwe). For the most part they were in their early 20s and had recently finished their National Service and were ready to embark on what they felt was a great adventure. They were all full of enthusiasm and energy and I always hoped that they made a success of their lives there.

In those days many of the passengers who had never flown before were very nervous at the prospect. Sometimes a passenger would come on board, literally shaking with fear, and of course, we would do everything we could to help them overcome their anxiety. Taking the time to have a few words with them usually helped and, soon after take-off, I would stop to talk to them but often they were so nervous that they didn't reply. However, one thing I found very useful was to say, 'Look,' pointing out of the window, 'you can see the English coast. That's Sussex, near Newhaven. We shall be crossing the coast in a few minutes and then very soon, if you look ahead, you'll be able to see France.' More often than not, the passenger would become so interested in watching the English coast getting nearer and nearer and then slipping beneath us, and then looking ahead to catch a first sight of the French coast, that they forgot their nerves.

Even if the flight had taken off in the evening and the land below us was in darkness, you could still point to the strings of lights that marked towns along the coast of England. And when flying over the Alps at night, the sight could be breathtaking. I remember one night flight in particular; it was mid-January, the Alps below us were covered in a lot of snow, and there was a full moon. I announced to the passengers that I was going to turn out the cabin lights for a few minutes so that they could all enjoy this spectacular sight.

Sights like this helped to make the flight 'special' for passengers and I was always pleased when someone, who had been very nervous when they first boarded, left the aircraft saying 'Thank you so much – I really enjoyed the flight and now I'm looking forward to my flight home.'

Quite often some passengers were so nervous that they would be sick. They were usually embarrassed when this happened and so, without saying anything, we would remove the used "sick bag" and replace it with a new one, and hand them some damp paper towels to wipe their face. I had been airsick myself so I could sympathise with them and understood the feeling of just wanting to get off the aircraft and never fly again! One day, as an Air Hostess took away a used "sick bag" the passenger called her back. 'My teeth came out when I vomited, and they are in that bag,' he said, and she had to retrieve his dentures for him. No… it wasn't always a glamorous job!

In contrast to these first-time nervous passengers, quite often we had unaccompanied children on board who were very well-travelled. When I stopped to chat and make sure they were all right, I would discover that their parents lived in Africa or the Far East and, far from this being their first flight alone, they were used to flying back and forth to school in England several times each year. Some of those children were seasoned world travellers by the time they were ten years old! When we stayed overnight with the passengers, which we still did on the West African route, unaccompanied children were always placed in the care of the air hostess. Luckily, I only ever had children in my care who were very well behaved and didn't try to wander off sightseeing on their own in the evenings. If we were staying overnight in a town, such as Las Palmas, it sometimes happened that one or two of them would say that they wanted to buy a present for their parents or grandparents, and so I would go with them to the shops in the town.

One day, when I was talking to some of the passengers, an elderly woman told me that her father had been in the Diplomatic Corps, posted to St Petersburg before the First World War. Of course that city is now called St Petersburg again, but at the time I talked to this passenger, it was still called Leningrad, which was behind the so-called "Iron Curtain", and the name didn't change back to St Petersburg for several years. She described garden parties and balls at embassies that she'd attended in 1910 and 1911 when the Tsar and Tsarina were often guests. They and their whole family were, of course, assassinated just a few years later.

On another flight, an elderly man who was a passenger asked if it would be possible to go up to the flight deck and look around. 'I was in the Royal Flying Corps in the First World War,' he told me, 'and I'd really like to see what the cockpit looks like now.' I told him that I'd check with the captain and I was sure that there would be time during the flight for him to go "up front". Later, after he had been to the flight deck and was back in his seat, I asked if he'd enjoyed looking around. 'Oh yes,' he said, 'but all those instruments they have to watch! I only recognised two of them – the one that showed the altitude and the one that showed the speed!' I told him that my own grandfather had been in the Royal Flying Corps in the First World War, and I asked him about some of his experiences.

He said that when he had first qualified as a pilot, he had come home on leave, feeling very proud of himself, and he showed off to his mother and her friends by telling them about the reconnaissance flights he'd made over the German lines. His mother became very upset, worrying that the Germans might shoot him down. 'But,' he told me, 'I said "Mother, don't worry. Jerry can't hit us. We're doing 30 miles an hour".'

When one of my friends was working on a flight to Bahrein, as usual she spent some time chatting to the passengers. A woman who was a resident in Bahrein was particularly friendly, and asked how long the crew would be staying in Bahrein. When my friend said that she would have a whole day off there, the woman invited her to visit her home. 'Do please come and have tea with me. I will invite some of my friends who will be very interested to talk to you and I will send a car and driver to bring you to the house.' My friend accepted the invitation and next afternoon a Rolls Royce came to the hotel and took her to "the house", which turned out to be like a small palace set in magnificent grounds. At the end of the afternoon, when my friend was ready to return to the hotel, the hostess said, 'Before you go, I want to give you a small souvenir of this afternoon.' She opened a box that a servant had placed beside her and rummaging through it she said, 'English ladies always like sapphires... they match their blue eyes,' and she handed my friend a very beautiful sapphire and diamond ring!

I was never invited to visit anywhere so palatial, or given such an amazing gift, but on flights to and from Nairobi, I had met the same woman passenger several times. She and her husband owned a coffee "shamba" (the Swahili word for "farm") in the White Highlands of Kenya, several hours' drive from Nairobi, and she invited me to visit her there. Because I only ever had one day free in Nairobi, which didn't give me enough time to get there and back, she asked me to come and stay for a short holiday. I accepted the invitation but unfortunately, she was killed in a road accident before I could visit her "shamba".

Whenever we landed at Khartoum at night, because of the lack of light pollution and the clear air, we would always see several shooting stars. Everyone enjoyed this sight; there is something magical about seeing a shooting star, and we would always see not just one or two, but several.

On one occasion, when one of our routine passenger flights travelling north from Entebbe towards Benghazi was scheduled to land at Khartoum to refuel, they found that for once the skies were not crystal clear because a sandstorm had blown up making visibility too poor for the aircraft to land. They had to divert to El Obeid, also in the Sudan, to pick up the needed fuel. Unfortunately, there was no aircraft fuel at the airport at El Obeid and it had to be brought from the nearby town; 1100 gallons were carried in 4-gallon cans. Refuelling from those small cans took four and a half hours!

Khartoum once presented us with a very unusual landing situation. One day, with a full load of passengers, we started our descent into the airport there. It was a perfectly clear day, with visibility of many miles and we got lower and lower. Everything was completely normal and I was just about to take my own seat for landing when suddenly the engines went to full power and we zoomed off up again. I went up to the front to find out what was happening so that I could tell the passengers, and I found the captain was shouting at the control tower, 'There are camels on the runway. Get a truck out there and clear them off!' He turned to me and said, 'Let the passengers know that we had to abort the landing because of camels on the runway and tell them we're going round again, while the runway is cleared.' I made an announcement telling the passengers what had happened, and in a few minutes we started our descent again. We got lower and lower, and suddenly... ZOOM! Up we went again. I went back up to the front and this time I found the captain red in the face with rage and shouting a few choice words to the control tower to the effect that 'Those ****ing camels are back again!'

Camels wandering in the desert near Khartoum have undoubtedly been a common sight for many centuries; a UFO hovering over Khartoum is not a common sight! One of our freight planes (a York) was descending to land at Khartoum with four men on the crew who had all been flying for at least 15 years. Suddenly the captain and first officer pointed ahead to an "object" hovering over the airport and asked each other, 'What's *that*?' The other two men on the crew (a flight engineer and a radio officer-navigator) also looked ahead and were equally amazed by the sight. The captain called the Khartoum control tower which, at that time, had all British staff, and asked, 'What's hovering over your runway?' The answer came back, 'We don't know what it is. We can all see it, but it's not showing on our radar screens.' They all described what they were seeing as a "classic flying saucer shape" and it was hovering, just a few hundred feet high, absolutely still. Obviously, our aircraft could not land, so it went into a circuit around the airport with all four men on the crew watching "it" the whole time. Suddenly they all shouted, 'It's starting to move...' And the radio officer who told me this story said, 'It started to move very slowly, and then suddenly it went off at such a speed that it left a blur on your eyeballs.' The men on the crew, with their many years of flying experience, were all well aware of the tricks that light can play, but all four were adamant that this was no trick sighting and was certainly not a weather balloon because of the speed at which it moved off. All four men made an official report of the incident, as did the staff in the Khartoum control tower.

Chapter 5

'We Regret the Delay...'

For the most part, at the time I was flying, the pilots, radio officers and flight engineers were able to walk back through the cabin to stretch their legs, because in those days, although some bombs had been exploded in London and other cities in England, and we were warned to be alert at all times to watch for bags or packages left unattended, there was not the terrorist threat that there is today. As well as actual bombs, there were also quite a number of hoaxes when telephone calls would be made claiming that there was a bomb at a certain location.

One day, we'd flown up to Manchester to pick up a group of passengers who were going to Majorca. Soon after take-off from Manchester, the light went on in the galley indicating that I should go up to the flight deck. When I got there the captain told me, 'We've just been radioed that someone has phoned Manchester Airport saying that there is a bomb on the Hunting-Clan Viscount that has just taken off for Majorca. We have to go into Heathrow for the aircraft to be checked. Don't tell the passengers it's a bomb scare… tell them anything you like to explain the diversion into Heathrow.' I couldn't think what I could say to the passengers but I knew that I certainly didn't want them to be scared by what I was convinced was just a hoax. So I made an announcement that really said nothing. 'Ladies and gentlemen, the captain has just told me that we have been called into London's Heathrow Airport. I don't know the reason for this, but I can assure you that we will take off again with as little delay as possible. After we've landed, you will be taken to the restaurant where you will be served afternoon tea.'

I felt nothing but irritation at this delay. I was quite certain it was a hoax and I was sure that someone had made the telephone call thinking it was a huge joke to play on friends who were passengers on board. However, just as we made the final turn to land at Heathrow Airport, I looked out of a window and saw the runway had fire engines and ambulances lined up along each side of it, waiting for us, and I suddenly thought, 'Oh my God… this could be *real*.' As soon as we came to a halt, security people rushed on board, and one of them asked, 'Who is the senior air hostess?' I said, 'I am.' 'Right,' he said, 'send your other girl with the passengers. You stay on board with us and help search the aircraft.' Search the aircraft? I hadn't a clue what a bomb might look like. Needless to say, my instinct that it was a hoax was correct, and after about an hour on the ground we took off again for Majorca.

It was rare for passengers to be rude, and if they were, it was usually because they were nervous when they first boarded the flight or perhaps a delay had made them irritable. No matter what the reason, delays are always a nuisance but sometimes passengers would be unreasonable, and it almost seemed as if they blamed us, the crew, even if it was bad weather that was causing the delay. One day, when a woman said to me 'I'm furious about this delay. I'm going to a big party in London tonight, and now I shall be late,' I felt like replying 'Oh I do understand how you feel because I am going to a party too tonight… and as it's my engagement party I'd really like to be there!' (I did get back in time for the party, but I didn't marry that man!)

On another occasion we were delayed because we burst two tyres on the main wheels of a Britannia on landing. Both tyres had to be replaced, of course, which meant that the aircraft had to be jacked up while it was done. After an hour a man complained to me about the length of time it was taking and I started to explain about having to jack up the aircraft. 'I know, I know,' he said irritably, 'but I can jack up my car to change a wheel a lot quicker than this.' I did tell him that this was a rather more complicated situation, in that a Britannia weighs over 145 tons.

Usually, however, it was best just to keep smiling and say as little as possible, except for something soothing like 'I've had a word with the flight engineer and he tells me that they are putting extra men on the repair crew, so we'll be away as quickly as possible.' Or 'The captain says we shall be away soon, and as we have a tail wind we will make up time on the journey.'

Sometimes the delay was caused by some technical fault or a problem with the aircraft, and in those circumstances we would tell the passengers as little as possible – certainly nothing that might alarm them. The "reason" (not necessarily the truth) that we gave most often to explain the delay was, 'We have a fault with the radio.' And, as far as possible, we didn't tell the passengers that there might be anything wrong unless and until we knew for sure that there *was* a problem. Then we would give them instructions about clearing everything away from the area around their feet, tell them how to sit and brace for the landing, and remind them where the emergency exits were. On one occasion when we knew that we were going to have a problem on landing, we made sure that all the exits were clear, and that everything stowed in the overhead racks was secure or taken down. The passengers were reminded of emergency instructions, and were told how to brace, and I was amazed when a young woman stopped me, and held out her baby saying, 'Would you hold him for the landing?' Apart from the fact that I, like all the cabin crew in those circumstances, would be fully occupied after landing, getting everybody off as quickly as possible, I can't imagine ever giving my baby to somebody else to hold in such a situation.

Even a normal landing can present unexpected problems – a heavy landing, or a skid, or a burst tyre – and we always checked to make sure that a passenger travelling with a baby had not fastened the seat belt around herself *and* the baby. The belt should be fastened only around the passenger and the baby should then be held outside the seat belt. If a problem upon landing causes a jolt, this would force the passenger forward, causing injuries to the baby if they were both enclosed by the same seat belt. We also had to remind people to hold the baby firmly while we were landing because often, having fastened their own seat belt, they would then bounce the baby up and down on their lap. If any problem occurred upon landing, and the baby wasn't being held firmly, it could be thrown out of its mother's arms and go flying through the cabin, injuring not only itself but also anybody it hit.

On a flight to an airport in Norway, we started our descent and the captain lowered the landing gear. Three green lights should come on in front of him, to show that both main wheels and the nose wheel are all down and locked in position. On this day, the green light for the nose wheel did not come on. The captain buzzed for me to go up front and he explained what was happening. 'It's possible – and most likely – that the light bulb has failed. But it is also possible that the nose wheel isn't down properly. We are going to fly low around the control tower and they are going to take a look at us.' He added, 'Don't say anything to the passengers until we know more.' We flew around the control tower three times, and then the captain called me up again to let me know that the people in the control tower had looked at us through binoculars and they said that our nose wheel *was* down but, of course, they couldn't tell if it was locked in position. It was decided not to say anything to the passengers and hope that the only thing wrong was a burned-out light bulb. In fact, everything was fine, the nose wheel *was* down and locked, and we landed without incident. As the passengers were leaving the aircraft, several of them said to me, 'Do please thank the captain for flying around several times. We had a wonderful view of the fjords and the surrounding countryside.'

Another landing in a Scandinavian country presented a quite different situation. We were flying into Malmo in Sweden and none of the crew had ever been there before, but with maps and radio contact with the air traffic controllers they navigated us easily to Malmo. As we approached the airport, the captain called the control tower for instructions and was told to descend to a certain level, and then continue on the flight path. After a few minutes he called the control tower again, and confirmed that he was now at the height they'd decreed and that he had the runway in sight. Their next instruction was to 'follow the Scandinavian Airlines DC6 in....' The captain and the first officer both looked around, and neither could see a DC6, or any other aircraft that they could 'follow in'. The captain called again, saying that they had no sight of a DC6, but the runway was dead ahead and they were now down to an even lower level. Immediately the answer came back, 'Pull up, pull up, pull up! You are about to land at a restricted military airport which is 30 miles west of us.'

No matter how important the passenger, delays can and do happen. Because I stayed in Entebbe so often, I became friendly with a young woman who lived there and worked at the airport. One day she told me about her experience when the late Queen Mother's flight had been delayed at Entebbe Airport. The Queen Mother was returning to England from an official visit to Australia, and was being flown home on the Australian airline QANTAS. When the plane made a refuelling stop at Entebbe, an engine fault was discovered that meant a delay of several hours. The Queen Mother was told about this, and she was taken to the Lake Victoria Hotel where a suite had been made ready for her. Unfortunately the repairs to the engine took longer than expected, because the part that was needed had to be flown out to Uganda. When it was explained to Her Majesty that they would not now be able to leave until the next day, she asked to be taken back to "her" aircraft. She said it had been made very comfortable for her and she would prefer to spend the night there rather than at the hotel. So, accompanied by a lady-in-waiting and her personal security staff, she spent the night aboard the delayed QANTAS aircraft at the airport. When the replacement part arrived, it was fitted, but other problems were then discovered and eventually the Queen Mother spent three days living at the Lake Victoria Hotel in the daytime, and returning to "her" aircraft to sleep each night.

After the first day, when it was realised that the delay would be longer than expected, it had been suggested to her that she could proceed to London aboard the BOAC aircraft that had been "shadowing" her flight. She said no thank you, she'd prefer to stay with the QANTAS aircraft and crew that she'd started off with.

One morning, just before she left the airport for the short drive to the hotel, the lady-in-waiting said to the woman who told me this story that the Queen Mother would like to get her nails repainted. 'Is there a manicurist at the airport or the hotel?' she asked. My friend said no, there wasn't but because the Queen Mother looked so dejected, she decided to be very bold and said, 'If it would help... I'd be happy to do the best I can.' The Queen Mother accepted the offer and during the time my friend spent "doing her nails" the Queen Mother was very chatty, asking about my friend's husband and children, and talking about her own family.

Sometimes a delay can be unexpectedly lucky. I left London taking a holiday charter flight to Agadir in Morocco. When we stopped to refuel at Gibraltar, we found that a fault had developed which meant that we had to stay there overnight. The passengers were, not surprisingly, quite disgruntled to find that their stay in Agadir would be cut short because of a delayed arrival. Next morning, however, before we left the hotel we heard news that made all of us realise that the delay in Gibraltar had been a blessing in disguise. During the night an earthquake had struck Agadir and the hotel in which we should all have spent the night had collapsed completely.

Looking through my Log Book, I find that Christmas was a time when I often had delays. Just before Christmas 1957 I worked on our regular flight to Accra, but on arrival there it was found that an engine problem had developed, and it took several days to get the necessary parts flown out to us and then have them fitted. As each day passed, it seemed more and more likely that Christmas Day would be spent with curry on the beach and not around the Christmas tree at home! The situation was not improved by the hotel music system playing Bing Crosby singing "I'll Be Home For Christmas" almost continuously!

One year, I arrived back in London just after midnight on Christmas Eve having flown from Adelaide, Australia. We had had delays all along the route and I'd worked for over 58 hours without a break. We had flown out to Australia to pick up a film unit that had been making "The Sundowners". The two stars of the film, Deborah Kerr and Robert Mitchum, had flown to California once they had finished filming so they were not on our flight back to London.

Both going to and returning from Australia, we followed a route that took me to a place that very few people, even airline crews, have seen – the Cocos Keeling Islands. (Nowadays they are called simply: Cocos Islands.) I have never met anyone else who has been there. Lying almost exactly halfway between Sri Lanka and Perth, Western Australia, on a map the Cocos Keeling Islands look like tiny dots in the middle of a vast ocean. The largest of the islands is only just big enough for a runway that can handle a DC6.

On the way out to Australia, before we left Sri Lanka, we had, of course, filed a flight plan. This showed that we would be flying through the night and would arrive at the Cocos Keeling Islands soon after dawn for refuelling. Somehow that flight plan was never put into the system, or activated, because the people in the Cocos Keeling Islands had no notice that we were on the way. Throughout the night our radio-navigator called the control tower there without getting any response. They had closed for the night and nobody would go on duty till next morning! He had to navigate by dead reckoning without any radio beacon to help guide him, and he did so with such superb skill that we descended to land there at exactly the time shown on our misplaced flight plan.

These islands looked like a perfect tropical paradise island – pale golden sand beaches, fringed by palm trees, and the sea was a bright turquoise blue with white surf breaking over a reef, outside which the water was a deeper blue. But the scene was not as idyllic as it appeared. There were notices saying "Do not walk on the beach" (there were stinging and biting insects in the sand) and "Beware, basking sharks".

A third story that relates to Christmas took place in 1958. Early on the morning of Christmas Day, I was scheduled to take out a flight carrying a group of passengers who were going to Paris for a short break. We should have taken off from London at about 8am but were delayed because of fog, and we waited at the airport hoping that it would lift. Eventually we had a message from the weather office saying that we should board our passengers and be ready for take-off, because it looked as if a short break in the weather was coming. As they had forecast, there *was* a short break, the fog lifted and we were one of only two aircraft that took off from Heathrow that day. Almost immediately after we'd taken off, the fog came down again so that by the time we landed in Paris, Heathrow had closed down again. In the hope that there might be a break in the weather later on and we would be able to fly home, we stayed at the airport rather than go to a hotel. Eventually, with still no improvement in the weather, we decided to have our Christmas dinner at the airport. I looked at the menu. 'Oh good... duck... lovely, I'll have that.' Unfortunately, when the duck came it was very tough and almost inedible, and I left most of it. When the waiter cleared away my plate he asked in his heavily accented English, 'Deed you enjoy zee durck?' 'No,' I said, 'it was very tough.' He gave that well known Gallic shrug and said, 'Bien sur, madam. Durck ees always turf.' Since then, I've never understood the enthusiasm for French cuisine!

Chapter 6

That's Show Business!

Sometimes we would be "on duty" but not flying. One such occasion was when the airline chartered some coaches to take travel managers from major companies to visit Farnborough Air Show. An air hostess was on board each coach and served coffee, tea or drinks from a bar that had been fitted on to the coach. Serving these drinks on a moving coach was a much more hazardous operation than serving them on a flight because a coach, travelling along a road, bumps about far more than any aircraft. But the passengers were determined to enjoy their day out to the full and even though we'd set off fairly early in the morning, they wanted their gin or whisky. Nowadays you hear about "air rage" and passengers who have to be restrained because they have drunk heavily before boarding the flight, and then continue to drink until the cabin crew refuse to serve them any more alcohol. I can truthfully say that I don't recall a single instance of any passenger becoming abusive or unpleasant because of drinking too much. Oh well... of course, the occasional man would have had enough to drink in the bars at the airport before boarding, so that by the time the flight was under way, he considered himself a great romantic fellow and would make a few drunken lurches at the air hostesses. But nothing worse than that; certainly nothing that could be termed "air rage".

Somehow, despite bumping about on the coach, I managed not to spill any drinks on that trip to Farnborough although I have occasionally spilled a drink on a passenger on the aircraft. I think it is inevitable that somehow, some time, spills will happen if there is a sudden lurch as the aircraft hits an air pocket or if you are flying through stormy weather. If you are pouring coffee or tea, or handing a drink to a passenger just when the aircraft gives a "bump" it always seems that the liquid splashes on to the passenger's lap. On two or three occasions I've rushed to the galley to get a cloth intending to wipe up a spill, but when I came back and saw where the liquid had landed on a man's lap, I've handed him the cloth saying, 'I think you may prefer to take care of this yourself, sir.' Once a full pot of freshly made, very hot coffee tipped into a young man's lap, and I've often thought that I might have stopped the continuation of his family line right then and there!

Another "on duty but not flying" day came about when Joyce Darbyshire (who had joined the airline the same day as I did) and I were at London's Heathrow Airport to take part in a film. It was called "Friends and Neighbours" and starred Arthur Askey who was a well known comedian at

58

that time. The "friends" in the title were supposed to be a group of Russians who were visiting England to stay with ordinary families, and Joyce and I played the parts of air hostess and ground hostess, as the "Russian visitors" left the aircraft. I stood at the aircraft door steps saying, 'goodbye…' 'goodbye...' 'goodbye…' to each of them, then they went down the steps and Joyce, as the ground hostess, escorted them away from the aircraft. This was obviously a simple, straightforward scene to film, but it took several hours as take after take was done. In between takes, all the "passengers" and I went back on the plane and sat in the cabin. They were all regular "extras" who had previously worked together on a number of films so they all knew each other, and they wondered why they'd never met me before and they wanted to know what other films I'd worked on? Why hadn't they ever seen me around the studios? I explained that I wasn't an "extra" but that I was an air hostess. 'You're a *real* air hostess?' While I was fascinated to see "the other side of the camera" of the film world, they were all intrigued to ask all sorts of questions about being an air hostess, what the job actually entailed, what were passengers really like, where I'd been and so on. When the director finally decided that he had the scene filmed to his satisfaction, they asked Joyce and I to pose for some publicity stills. When the photographer had finished, we both turned to leave, but as we were waving goodbye to the people we'd met, someone rushed up and said, 'You can't go… you haven't been paid.' Both Joyce and I were surprised and said that we hadn't expected to be paid but we were told that Equity rules dictated that we must be paid the daily rate as "extras". When the film was shown in cinemas, I went with my parents to see it, and it was just like the old saying "If you blinked you'd have missed me." After all the hours spent filming the scene, Joyce and I were on screen for a total of perhaps two or three minutes.

After I'd been flying for a couple of years, the airline started to send one or two of us out to give talks to various clubs who wanted a speaker at their meetings. As it was publicity for the airline, we were expected to tell our audiences something about Hunting-Clan and what sort of flights we offered, and then just ad lib any stories we liked about how we'd joined the airline, our training, details about people we'd met and places we'd visited. The first time I gave such a talk I was so nervous that as the chairwoman introduced me I felt my knees turn to jelly and I remember the thought going through my head that when I stood up to walk to the microphone, my legs would buckle under me. Somehow, I managed to conquer those nerves, delivered my talk, took questions at the end, and then as I sat down to a round of applause and a speech of thanks, I realised how much I'd enjoyed doing it! In that moment I was hooked on "public speaking" and many years after I'd left the airline I continued to give talks to any groups that wanted a speaker, not talking about "being an air hostess" but raising funds for an animal charity.

Recently the wheel has turned full circle and now when I give a talk to groups such as the Women's Institute, the Townswomen's Guild, or Probus, it is about my days as an air hostess, over half a century ago. Of course, the talk is called "Before There Were Trolley Dollies".

At the end of those talks, I always ask the audience if they have any questions. One of the most frequently asked questions is "We've always heard that there were a lot of affairs between the men and women on airline crews when you were away from England. Can you tell us just what went on while you were away?" Well, given that we were away from home for two or three weeks at a time, and the men were mostly in their middle or late 30s and spent all their off-duty time with attractive, young women, I suppose it isn't surprising that quite a lot did "go on". But I must have been very naïve when I first started flying because when the captain on another crew invited me out for dinner I was happy to accept. He was a good conversationalist with a great sense of humour and we spent a very pleasant evening. As we were chatting over coffee after dinner, he said, 'Oh well, I'm on the crew that flies back to England tomorrow. When I get home I expect the lawn will need cutting and there will be all sorts of problems in the house that I'll have to deal with.' In my naivety I thought that he must live with his parents and was taking care of the garden and household chores for them. If he were not single, surely he wouldn't have invited me out for dinner? I asked him about "home" and who lived there, and I was absolutely dumbstruck when he said, 'My wife, of course, and the children.' Yes! I certainly *was* naïve!

But maybe I wasn't unusual for that day and age... maybe we were all rather more gullible than young women are nowadays. I remember at least two occasions when air hostesses met men who were on business trips overseas and, as the men would be back in England before the air hostess was scheduled to arrive, they had given the girls their phone numbers in England and made them promise to phone. 'You will phone, won't you, just as soon as you get back to England...' In both cases the telephone numbers were completely fictitious; the men obviously had no intention of having the girls get in touch with them back in England! Another girl met an Englishman who was working in (what was then) Southern Rhodesia. He proposed marriage to her, told her that he would be back in England in a few weeks, and suggested that in the intervening time she should look around at houses that were for sale and if she found one she liked, he would buy it on his return to England. He told her 'You can look at houses up to £12,000', which was an enormous sum to pay for a house in the late 1950s. Need I add that not only did he have no intention of marrying her, but he was already married!

But apart from "goings on" I also tell audiences that I know of three marriages that took place between pilots and air hostesses who had met down the route. And by strange coincidence, I also know of three divorces that happened because of "what went on" when crews were slipping. Then I always add, 'Yes, of course, I *could* tell you a lot...' (at this point the audience visibly leans forward) '...but I'm very well aware of the law of slander, and I'm not going to!' However, I do mention that the airline issued a manual that listed the airline's rules governing all crew behaviour and instructed us as to how we should handle any eventuality. For instance – just like the Guards at Buckingham Palace changing from their grey winter coats to their scarlet summer jackets on a specific date – the manual instructed us when to stop wearing black winter gloves and start wearing white summer gloves; and it specified at what point down the route we should start to wear our "tropical uniform" instead of the "European uniform". In that manual there was also an instruction that read: "At all times, the air hostess comes directly beneath the captain." Perhaps you could say that this particular instruction was taken too literally in some cases!

Air hostesses were often asked to appear at special events and, of course, this was a good way of promoting Hunting-Clan or, as it later became, British United Airways. Sometimes we were asked to pose for photographs for aviation and travel magazines and on one occasion I was photographed both alone and with another air hostess for postcards that went on sale at several airports in West Africa.

A "marketing and promotion" trip to Holland was organised by the airline and I was one of three air hostesses who went there with the airline's sales and marketing managers. For several days we visited travel agents and large businesses in Amsterdam, Rotterdam, Delft and other cities, promoting our "businessmen's special" flights. These flights left England early in the morning and the "businessmen" would have breakfast on board, spend the day having meetings and conducting business in Holland,

and then fly back to England in the evening, having their dinner on board. The journey from Rotterdam or Amsterdam to Gatwick took 65 to 70 minutes and during that time we sold duty-free cigarettes to the passengers, served drinks and dinner, followed by coffee and liqueurs. No, don't ask how we managed to do all that in just over an hour!

Looking back, I'm not sure how much business our "flag showing" visit to Holland generated for the airline, but I do remember that everybody – the sales people, the potential clients we visited, and we air hostesses – all had a wonderful time; each day was filled with laughter and jokes. One Dutch businessman who was very serious and quite dour when we first met him, quickly relaxed and by the time we left I remember his parting words were 'I shall tell everybody what jolly girls there are in England.'

On the whole, almost everybody – men and women, aircrew and ground staff – who worked for Hunting-Clan and BUA had a terrific sense of humour and we were a genuinely happy group. The notice board in the Operations Room was often good for a laugh when someone (always anonymous!) had scribbled a humorous – frequently ribald – comment on an official notice or announcement. One day, someone had pinned a magazine article to the notice board which said that being an air hostess was a wonderful job… "These young women travel the world, staying in the best hotels, sightseeing and shopping in cities on every continent. And the job is a great way to meet a husband."

Beside the words "a husband" somebody had scrawled "Whose?"

As I've mentioned, a few pilots and air hostesses did get married, but not many, and I only know of one marriage between an air hostess and a passenger.

Another notice that went on the board announced that new-style uniform blouses were to be issued. So that orders could be placed in appropriate numbers for each size, every air hostess's name was listed and we were asked to "indicate your bust size next to your name." Most of the girls had written in "32" or "34" but just one girl (who happened to be one of the prettiest of all the air hostesses) had written in "40". Somebody (perhaps the same wag who had wondered *whose* husband we would meet) had written one word: "COR!"

When we amalgamated with other airlines to form British United Airways, and then as the airline grew bigger, obviously there were many more employees. For the first few years that I was flying, almost everybody knew everybody else, but after British United Airways was formed and then expanded, sometimes you went on duty for a flight and found that you were working with another air hostess, and even a whole crew, that you'd never met before. But even if you were flying with an air hostess you hadn't met, you soon got to know each other very well. After all, you weren't just working together, but if you were on a long trip you were also spending all your off-duty time together too. This wasn't just a job; it was a way of life. Looking back, it seems surprising that there was never any

65

bitchiness or jealousy between "the girls" and some of the friendships formed then have lasted to this day even though many of us have spent years living in different parts of the world. Once every two years, there is a reunion of British United Airways air crews, both men and women. Husbands and wives aren't invited, and we all get together for lunch and chat, reminiscing about "the old days" – 50 or more years ago – and assuring each other that, 'You really haven't changed... you look just the same.'

Of all the "special flights" that I worked on, I remember one when we were chartered to take a film unit to East Africa but it is the return flight that really stands out in my memory. When I checked in for the outward bound flight to Nairobi, I asked if anybody knew anything about the film that was to be made? 'Yes,' I was told, 'it's a Tarzan film.' 'Oh,' I started to say, 'Johnny Weissmuller...' I remembered him from my childhood. The Operations staff laughed at me and said, 'No, dear, Johnny Weissmuller was a *long* time ago. Tarzan is now being played by an actor called Gordon Scott.' I'd never heard of Gordon Scott and I didn't know any of the other actors on board. I didn't recognise their faces or their names. About a month later I went out to Nairobi and picked up the same film unit and brought them back to England. The passengers were mostly the "technical" people who took care of lighting, sound, and cameras. Sy Weintraub, the producer of the film, was also on board, as well as the same actors who had flown out with us a month or so earlier.

As it was a "special flight" a menu had been printed with the details of the charter, and at some point one of these menus was handed round and the actors signed it. One of the young actors handed the (folded closed) menu back to me and said, 'I've put a special message in there for you, Miss Austin.' I said 'Thank you', put it in my flight bag, and forgot about it because I was too busy during the approach to London to look at it. I didn't remember it till next morning when I was at home. I opened up the menu and looked inside and I found that the "message" read:

"Miss Austin, I love you, Sean Connery."

(Yes I still have that menu!)

Angela in Hunting-Clan uniform, 1957

Angela in Hunting-Clan uniform, 1958

Hunting-Clan air hostesses (Angela far left) in tropical uniform

The interior of a Viking aircraft, 1957

Hunting-Clan Viscount aircraft, with the famous red tail

Angela with young chimpanzee passenger at Entebbe, Uganda

Angela holding koala bear in Adelaide, South Australia

Angela with apes on "The Rock", Gibraltar

View from the cockpit of a Viscount, coming in to land at Entebbe, Uganda

The "Sea of Sand", Sahara

Lions in Nairobi Game Park

Murchison Falls, Uganda, where "The African Queen" was filmed

Sleeping quarters at Murchison Falls Game Reserve

The beach, Cocos-Keeling Islands

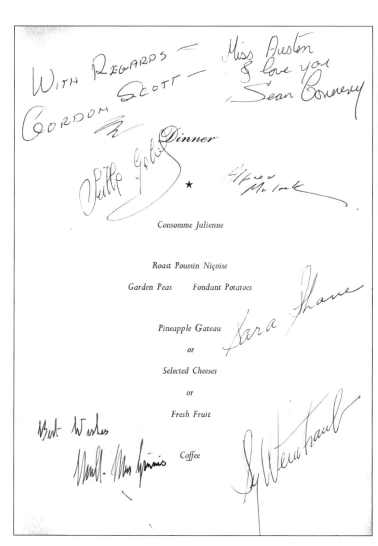

With Regards —
Gordon Scott —
Miss Buston
& love you
Sean Connery

Spille Gola Dinner

★

Consomme Julienne

Roast Poussin Niçoise

Garden Peas   Fondant Potatoes

Pineapple Gateau

or

Selected Cheeses

or

Fresh Fruit

Coffee

Best Wishes

Menu signed by Sean Connery, declaring his love!

Angela at Benghazi, at the time when a harbour mine was named after her

Waiting for passengers - Angela and another air hostess in aircraft doorway

Angela with two other B.U.A. air hostesses in tropical uniform (wearing hated jockey caps, which only lasted for a few months)

Angela on aircraft steps at Entebbe, Uganda

Chapter 7

Four-footed Passengers

As an animal lover, some of my happiest memories concern animals that I "met" around the world. As I've already described, on occasion we would go and stay in the game reserves instead of at the hotel, and while staying at the lodge in a game park in Uganda, I chatted one evening to the chief game warden's wife. Apart from being in charge of the lodge, with its guest rooms and restaurant, and all the staff, she often found herself helping to care for orphaned or injured young animals that had been brought in by wardens who had found them while out in the game park. Sometimes the mother had died of natural causes; sometimes she'd been killed by poachers. But whatever the case, her youngsters needed care. When a baby elephant was brought in after its mother had been killed, it was examined and found to be healthy. It just needed to be kept in a secure area, fed, and its progress monitored until it was old enough and strong enough to be returned to its natural habitat. However, feeding it proved to be a problem. Various mixes of cow's milk and goat's milk were put into a large bottle with a very large teat, but the young elephant would not suck. The flavouring was altered, as was the temperature, but still the youngster refused to suck. Suddenly the chief game warden remembered that somewhere he'd read that an elephant's nipple has seven holes in it for the milk to come through, so they immediately punched more holes in the teat so that it had seven holes. The bottle was offered again to the baby elephant and triumph!!! He sucked!!! He thrived and grew and eventually he was successfully returned to the bush.

When we flew to Nairobi on one of our regular flights we had two nights there, which meant a whole day off. A young man who lived there always offered to take me to the Nairobi Game Park, which is just on the edge of the city. Each time we went there, it took a little while for me to "get my eye in". He would point and say, 'Look… Thomson's gazelle…' or 'Look, water buffalo…' but I would look in vain, not seeing whatever it was that he was trying to show me. After an hour or so my eyes would adjust, and I could see the various animals that he was pointing out. Zebras always make wonderful photographs, with their bold stripes against the background of shrubs and trees. Giraffes "pose" beautifully for you to take their photograph – they just stop chewing for a few seconds, turn their heads and look directly at you, standing in an elegant pose. Everybody who visits a game park always wants to see the lions. If you happen to pass another car, drivers will call to each other,

'Have you seen any lions?' or 'Where are the lions?' One day, as we were driving around Nairobi Game Park, the young man who had taken me there suddenly stopped the car and said, 'Look... right here!' And sure enough, a male and a female lion were right beside the track, within a few feet of us. Just before leaving the hotel I had put a new film into my camera, and for over an hour I snapped away from a distance of only about 10ft as these two lions went through their foreplay and eventually mated. Not too long after that event, Armand and Michaela Denis were passengers on board one of our flights. In the late 1950s they were very well known for making extremely popular wildlife films for television. When I had a chance to talk to them, I told them that I'd recently been close to a pair of lions who had mated, and I'd taken photographs of them. They weren't at all impressed. Armand turned to me and said, 'Mmmm... that's not surprising... lions are very promiscuous!'

On a trip to Australia, I did something that even Armand Denis would have had to admit was unusual; when I was in Adelaide in South Australia, I held a koala bear in my arms. Usually, koalas are animals that do not particularly like or respond to human contact. When we arrived in Adelaide, I told our agent at the airport that I'd love to see a real live koala bear. He said that he knew of a man who was trying to set up a small "petting zoo" where children could go and touch and hold animals, and he thought this man might have "tamed" a koala. Our agent made arrangements for me to go out to visit the man's small zoo next morning. When I got

71

there he told me that although it was very difficult to get any koalas to allow humans to touch them, he had one "old boy" that was starting to accept humans and he thought I might be able to hold him. We went into a compound of trees and bushes, and found the "old boy" clinging to one of the eucalyptus trees. I was told to stand absolutely still, keeping my arms straight down by my sides. 'Now,' said the man, 'I'm going to pick him up and pass him to you. Don't move and don't bring your arms up to try to hold him. Stand absolutely still as if you are a tree trunk.' He picked up the koala, held him for just a moment and then leaned towards me. I stood still and straight, arms by my sides as instructed. Suddenly the koala made a grab for me, swung himself over, and held on tightly, as if clinging to a tree. All toy stuffed koala bears I've ever seen have short, stubby, straight arms without any bend at the elbow. In real life, koalas have quite long arms that do bend at the "elbow" and they have very long black claws with which to hold on to tree trunks. After a couple of minutes of standing quite still, I gradually brought my arms up slightly so that I could hold him though only touching him very lightly, and somebody took my photograph. I'm glad I have that photograph because so few people in the world have actually held a koala bear.

When we flew to Gibraltar, usually we had just one night in the hotel and flew back early the next morning. We would leave the hotel earlier than necessary so that we could call in at the flower market because at that time, if you spent £1 on flowers, you had a bouquet that was almost bigger than you could easily carry. All the crew bought flowers to take home, which were then put into the hold. Sometimes, however, we would have two nights in Gibraltar, with a whole day free, and although the shopping was good (well-stocked shops and low prices – jewellery was a very good buy) I used to take the time to go up "The Rock" to where the famous apes lived. The first time I went, I was warned to hold on tightly to my handbag and my camera, because the apes would grab anything they could and make off with it. What I hadn't been warned about was that they just love to leap on to visiting humans and then "groom" their hair, and the only photograph I have of me with the apes is of one of them doing exactly that!

On one flight, in the hold we had carried a young cheetah that was going from East Africa to a zoo in Europe. After we arrived in London and all the passengers had disembarked, and after Customs had come on board and sealed the duty-free bar, I left the aircraft and there on the ground, just near the steps, was the cage containing the cheetah. He was sitting, looking around as if he was very interested in all that was happening, and was so beautiful that I couldn't resist going over. I crouched down in front of the cage and as the cheetah seemed very docile I ventured to put a hand through the bars of the cage and stroked the side of his neck. He obviously enjoyed this because he leaned slightly towards my hand and started purring... just like a domestic cat, only a lot louder.

Our freight planes, the Yorks, often carried animals, even large ones. Several times we carried quite well known racehorses that had been sold and were being taken to their new home abroad. Whenever animals were being transported on the Yorks, a trained animal handler would also be on board and, in case of any unfortunate event, they carried humane killers. We did have a racehorse that had to be destroyed when he went crazy during the flight and started kicking out violently, damaging the outer cabin walls. He had been tranquillized before departure, but the minimum sedative is always given because although you want a horse to be calm during the journey, you don't want it sedated so much that it "goes down" and this minimum sedative obviously wasn't enough.

One day, as we were preparing the aircraft for departure northbound from Entebbe, I was told that we would be carrying a young chimpanzee in the hold. Again it was being taken to a zoo in Europe. This chimpanzee was about 18 months old and had been rescued when its mother had died or been killed, and it had been reared by the staff at a game park in Uganda. As everything was being loaded into the hold, I saw the young chimpanzee arrive. I went down the steps and talked to the game warden – a woman – who had brought it to the airport. She was the person who had taken care of him ever since he had come to the game park and she was clearly upset to see him leave. She had been carrying the chimpanzee but when she put him down, I crouched down and held out my hand and he immediately grabbed it and held on very tightly. We held hands for a few minutes, and as he released my hand I noticed the palm of his hand; it had lines on it identical to those on a human hand, the lines that in palmistry are known as the head line, the heart line, and so on. Anyone who claimed to be able to read hands would have had no trouble reading this young chimp's palm and it gave me a slightly uneasy feeling to see how very much his palm resembled my own. It was even more poignant on a later flight when I saw that rhesus monkeys being carried to Europe for use in medical research also had these same "human looking" palms. I had no need of Charles Darwin to point out a connection between animals of the monkey world and human beings. The young chimp we were to carry on our flight this day was friendly and good natured, used to being around humans, and I could understand the game warden's distress at having to part from him.

The chimpanzee was put into a crate and it was loaded into one of the rear holds. I had to go back on the aircraft to ensure that all was ready for the passengers to board. On this day, when I went to check the rear lavatories I could hear the chimpanzee whimpering and crying. This was awful! Just then the captain came aboard. I asked him if he'd looked at the freight manifest and did he know about the young chimpanzee we had in the hold. Yes, he did. 'Come down to the back,' I said. 'Listen.' He listened and I asked, 'Isn't there any way we could carry him in the cabin? He is only used to being with people, and he's going to cry throughout the journey.' The captain thought for only a minute and then said, 'We don't have a full load. Clear a row of three seats right up at the front of the cabin, and we'll bring the crate up and strap it in there.' I couldn't have been more pleased… nor could the young chimpanzee! And what a useful "in flight tool" he proved to be. As it happened, there were quite a lot of children travelling with their parents on that flight and, as always, they soon became bored. I went to each of them and said, 'We have a young chimpanzee on board and if you are *very* good you can come up in turn, two at a time, and sit beside his cage.' It worked like a charm and several parents told me afterwards, 'The children have never been so well behaved on a flight, and never once did they say they were bored!'

Chapter 8

'I Don't Feel Very Well...'

When we used the Vikings and Yorks in the first year or two that I was flying, neither of these aircraft was pressurised. This meant that we did not fly above 10,000ft, except very occasionally when we would have to go higher to avoid thunderstorms. Aircraft get struck by lightning quite often and usually it doesn't give any cause for concern, but certainly major electrical storms and big cumulo-nimbus clouds would always be avoided if at all possible. When we had to go over 10,000ft, and even up to 12,000ft occasionally, usually passengers didn't feel any ill effects as they were sitting down and relaxing. As far as possible cabin crew would also sit down while we were at that altitude although, of course, if a meal had to be served or if a passenger needed your attention, you had to move about.

Because of not being pressurised, even when we were flying at our normal "below 10,000ft" level, some passengers felt the effects of lack of oxygen, and I have many notes in my log book showing "Gave oxygen". People who had any heart problems or emphysema or were asthmatic were especially susceptible to feeling breathless or even fainting.

One day, when I hadn't been flying very long, I was serving lunch to passengers on a Viking. I leaned across two women sitting in a row of three seats so that I could hand a meal tray to the woman sitting next to the window. 'I don't think she will want any lunch,' said the passenger sitting next to her, 'she said she didn't feel very well.' The woman appeared to be asleep. I handed the meal tray to a passenger on the other side of the aisle and then, leaning across the two women sitting in the same row as the woman who had said she didn't feel well, I touched her arm. 'Madam, are you all right?' I asked. No response. I shook her arm and asked again if she was all right. Again there was no response. I asked the two women sitting in that row to move out and stand in the aisle, so that I could get close to the non-responsive woman. Now I gripped her arm very firmly and shook it hard. 'Are you all right?' I asked very loudly. When I got no response this third time, I slipped my hand down her arm to the wrist and felt for the pulse. I couldn't feel any pulse! I took a deep breath and told myself to feel again… carefully. I did. I still couldn't feel any pulse. I put the tips of my fingers on the side of her neck, feeling for the carotid artery, but still I could not detect any pulse at all.

I went up to the flight deck and asked the captain to put up the "No Smoking" sign as I had to give oxygen. In those days there was no general announcement system on aircraft, so I had to go along row by row saying, 'Would you please not smoke – I have to give oxygen.' (Smoking, striking a match, or flicking a cigarette lighter while oxygen is being given could cause a fire.) I fetched the oxygen bottle and put the mask over the woman's nose and mouth and turned the flow of oxygen on "Full". The bellows, which should inflate and deflate as the patient breathes, just hung there motionless. I continued giving oxygen but the bellows still hung limply. At this point the captain came back and asked, 'Everything all right?' 'No,' I muttered to him quietly so that other passengers wouldn't hear. 'She's not breathing and I can't feel any pulse.' The look on his face spoke volumes; he was obviously thinking, 'New girl... probably doesn't know what she's doing,' and he leaned over, checked that the oxygen was flowing from the bottle, checked the bellows, which still weren't moving, and then he felt for a pulse at her wrist. His face was expressionless, 'Hmmm... I see what you mean,' he said in a very low voice. He stayed and I continued to give oxygen, and we both watched the dial going down as the supply was being used. When turned on fully, the oxygen bottle carried on an aircraft will last for about 15 to 20 minutes. I was already thinking, 'Where do I put a dead body? We have a full load and there's no space anywhere.' Our training had not covered such an eventuality! I was watching the dial on the bottle closely, and it was registering "Empty", when quite suddenly the woman sat up and pushed away the oxygen mask. She looked around and I asked, 'Do you feel all right?' 'Yes,' she said, 'except that I'm hungry. I'd like my lunch.' I've never served any passenger a meal more gladly! Don't ask me what happened. I don't know. I can't explain it. A few years ago, that captain was at one of our airline reunions, and I asked him if he remembered that event. 'Do I remember it?' he asked, 'It's something I'll never forget, nor will I ever understand what happened.'

That's the story of a passenger who "died" but came back to life, apparently feeling perfectly well and with no knowledge or recollection of anything being wrong with her.

On another occasion, I had a passenger who did die. We took off in a Viscount on what seemed to be a perfectly normal, scheduled flight from Entebbe heading north towards Benghazi with a refuelling stop at Khartoum on the way. During the refuelling process, it was discovered that we had a fuel pump problem. As it would take some time to get the necessary spare part and have it fitted, we took all the passengers over to what was at that time the only large hotel in Khartoum. The hotel was right across the road from the River Nile, and some of their "rooms" were actually cabins on a river boat, that was moored in front of the hotel. We took the passengers to the hotel at about breakfast time, and told them that we would not be leaving until some time in the evening and that they could have any food and drink that they wanted during the time we were at the hotel. That day was an exceptionally hot one, even for Khartoum, and in those days there was no air conditioning in the hotel's main building or on the boat, just ceiling fans.

Late in the afternoon, I was lying on my bed in just my underwear, with the ceiling fan turned on fully, trying in vain to get cool, when the telephone rang. It was the reception desk. 'One of your passengers has been taken ill. Would you come and see her.' As I struggled into my uniform, I asked, 'Which room is she in?' The ill passenger, Mrs B, was in one of the cabins on the river boat. I asked the receptionist to telephone the captain and tell him that we had a sick passenger, and also to telephone the second air hostess and ask her to come over to the river boat. When we arrived at the woman's cabin, a friend who was travelling with her was there. 'She is unconscious,' she said. As I was asking how long the woman had been unconscious, I put my hand out to touch her to see if I could rouse her and I almost jumped back. Her flesh was so hot to the touch it felt burning to my fingertips! The captain arrived and said that there were no ambulances in Khartoum, but the hotel staff had already called for a taxi so that we could, if necessary, take Mrs B to the hospital. She had been lying naked on the bunk in the cabin, with just a sheet covering her, so the other air hostess and I got the sheet wet, and then put it around her again, hoping that a wet sheet might help to cool her down a little. We went out to the waiting taxi and got into the back seat and two of the boat attendants carried the unconscious Mrs B out and laid her across our laps. When we arrived at the hospital, we were met by a young Sudanese doctor who had been trained in London and spoke excellent English. He took Mrs B's temperature. 'What is it?' I asked. 'It's 109 degrees,' he said. I couldn't believe it.

I'd never heard of anybody's temperature going that high. The doctor held out the thermometer and I looked. It did indeed read "109 degrees".

The captain went back to the hotel, so that he could keep in touch with the airport and be advised when our aircraft would be ready for us to leave. The other air hostess and I stayed at the hospital until we had a telephone call telling us that we should go back to the hotel, gather the passengers, and go to the airport ready for departure. By the time we reached the hotel, the captain had already taken a call from the Sudanese doctor telling him that Mrs B had died. We had to leave; our aircraft was ready for departure, and all the other passengers were anxious to continue their journey. On the flight north, I spoke to the woman who had been travelling with Mrs B and asked questions to try to find out as much as I could about her general state of health. Had she complained of feeling unwell before we arrived in Khartoum? How soon after reaching Khartoum had she first said she didn't feel well? My questions didn't elicit any useful information until suddenly, the friend told me that Mrs B had been dieting, and was taking in as little fluid as possible. Even in the heat of that day in Khartoum Mrs B had refused to drink at all. It seemed likely that she must have become dehydrated and been overcome by a form of heat stroke.

It wasn't only passengers that became ill. Sometimes crew members, too, came down with various ailments. During a stay in Entebbe, I was taken ill with food poisoning and after a day or two in the small local hospital,

I was flown home as a passenger. My illness had meant that I was unable to work as scheduled, and so the hostess who had worked on the flight coming into Entebbe had had to work straight on, in my place, without any rest.

At one time we had a number of crew members taken ill with some form of dysentery while "slipping" in Karachi. One day, I arrived in Karachi, having worked all the way from London, and was told that the senior hostess on the crew that was coming aboard was ill and I had to continue straight on to Bombay, Bangkok and Hong Kong! Because so many crew members had been taken ill in Karachi, once when I went there for a two-day "slip" I took a packet of biscuits off the aircraft with me to the hotel, and that was all I ate for the two days that I was there. I drank tea for those two days, thinking that as the water had been boiled to make the tea it would probably be safe. It proved to be a good decision because by having only tea and biscuits for those two days I managed to avoid a bout of dysentery.

Although there were (as there still are) very strict regulations governing the number of hours that the pilots could be on duty without a rest, at that time there were no regulations covering cabin crew. We could, and sometimes did, work incredibly long hours, such as the occasion when, having worked the flight from London to Karachi, I'd had to work straight on from Karachi to Hong Kong, which meant that I was on duty for a total of almost 36 hours. When pilots had worked their "allowed" number of hours, they would leave the aircraft and fresh pilots would come aboard, but the cabin crew would often have to continue working for several more hours.

Chapter 9

Food, Drink and Hotels

While the "durck" was "turf" in Paris and at Dijon I had an omelette which contained quite a lot of broken egg shells, I had other meals in France that were excellent, and there were many places around the world where the food was very good. Some places surprised everyone by having certain dishes that everybody enjoyed.

For example, nobody would ever expect to have food that was really delicious in the Sudan, but whenever we refuelled at Khartoum we would make for the airport restaurant and, despite the intense heat, which was only slightly mitigated by ceiling fans, we would all unfailingly order "Sudanese Soup". This was a delicious peanut soup that everybody enjoyed... although anybody who didn't like the taste of peanuts or peanut butter would hate it.

In Hong Kong there were so many restaurants of different nationalities that it was difficult to choose which national cuisine to have for dinner. There were several very good Russian restaurants in Hong Kong, and one evening when dining in one of the large luxury hotels I had something I'd never heard of until then, called a "carpetbagger steak" … this is a steak that has been stuffed with oysters.

In Entebbe the local fish, caught in Lake Victoria, was talapia which was delicious – just as well that it was delicious because (at that time, and things may have changed a great deal since then) I never saw any other kind of fish on any menu in Uganda!

But the fish I enjoyed the most anywhere in the world were the crayfish in Perth, Western Australia. I've never seen them so large, and never tasted them better! (Good on yer, cobbers!)

Anybody who has been to Malta will probably remember that the local bread is excellent – crusty on the outside, but light and fluffy inside. They must knead the dough for only a short time, because air holes are left in it and the baked loaf then has large "holes" or spaces in it.

In a hotel in Cairo, one morning I had ordered a glass of orange juice with my breakfast and when it was served it was such a bright red that I thought it was tomato juice! I called the waiter back, thinking a mistake had been made, and said 'I asked for orange juice, but….' 'Yes,' he said, 'this *is* orange juice, but it is from blood oranges.' And it was delicious.

I had heard stories about "huge" Australian breakfasts, so when I went to Australia and arrived in Perth in the early morning, having flown all night, it was perfect timing to see for myself just how "huge" the Australian breakfast was. I ordered a mixed grill and when it was served, it was on a very large platter rather than a plate. On the platter there was a decent sized steak, a lamb chop, bacon (several rashers), a couple of sausages, kidneys, tomatoes, scrambled eggs, mushrooms, and fried bread. Toast with honey and marmalade was also served, as well as fruit juice. I had a very hearty appetite, did justice to this enormous breakfast and ate everything on the platter. When the waitress came to clear away and saw that I'd eaten everything, she must have thought that perhaps I was still hungry because she asked, 'Would you like some more, dearie?'

The hotel in Perth, Western Australia where we stayed and where I had that magnificent breakfast was only five storeys high but I believe it was the tallest building in the city at that time. As I looked out of my bedroom window, in the centre of Perth, all I could see were mostly single-storey buildings, and almost all of them had corrugated iron roofs. When I see photographs of Perth nowadays, it bears absolutely no resemblance to the city in my memory. In fact, when I have seen pictures of present day Perth there are so many high rise buildings and skyscrapers, that I have thought the pictures were of Vancouver!

It was in that same hotel that I achieved a notable "first". As soon as all the crew had finished eating breakfast, we dispersed to our rooms for some much needed sleep. The captain said, 'See you all in the bar at... what... six o'clock?' After sleeping most of the day, I came down to join the crew and looked around the reception area. I couldn't see any signs pointing to a bar, but I could hear a lot of people talking and laughing, so I followed that sound to what I guessed (rightly) was the bar. I looked in and saw that the crew was already sitting there. As I walked over to join them I heard a strange thumping sound. I discovered afterwards that it was the sound of every man in the place putting down his tankard or glass – and putting it down with quite a thump! The captain looked up and saw me. 'Ah, there you are… what are you drinking?' I said I'd like a gin and tonic, and slid into a chair at the table with the rest of the crew. The captain turned to the barman to place the order. 'She can't drink in here,' said the barman. 'What?' asked the captain. 'Ladies aren't allowed to drink in the bar. She'll have to go to the lounge,' said the barman. There was complete silence in the bar. All conversation had stopped and not one man had picked up his glass and started drinking again. A short argument followed with the captain repeating the request for my gin and tonic and the barman insisting that "ladies" were not allowed to drink in the bar. Finally the captain stood up. 'She's one of the crew,' he said. 'She drinks with us and she'll have a gin and tonic.' The barman gave in and served my drink and thus I became the very first woman to drink in a bar in Australia.

The food in the hotel in Benghazi was pretty awful at that time. There's an old joke that asks, 'What is worse than finding a worm in an apple you're eating?' The answer is, 'Finding *half* a worm!' After eating lasagna for dinner one evening in Benghazi, I could ask a similar question. 'What is worse than finding a cockroach in your lasagna?' And the answer is, 'Finding *half* a cockroach!' After that experience, it took me several years before I could enjoy eating lasagna again.

Because we spent a lot of time in Benghazi and the food in the hotel and local restaurants was so bad, someone had the bright idea that we should all club together and buy two camping stoves and a couple of saucepans. We could then cook our own meals in one of the bedrooms. As the captain was always given the largest bedroom, the cooking was done there. During the day we would go to the market and the local shops and buy meat or poultry and vegetables, and then we'd throw everything into a big pan and cook up a stew or a curry. Rice or potatoes were cooked in the other large pan and in the time it took for everything to be cooked the two crews (the southbound one and the northbound one) would sit around, have a few drinks, chat and tell jokes. After we'd eaten, the dishes and pans were washed up in the bath. Cooking our own meals continued for several months until one of the captains put a stop to any further cooking by crews because, it was said, he claimed he'd got into his bath and sat on a fork. I don't know if this really happened or if it is an apocryphal story.

On a trip when we were able to spend two days in Athens, on the first day there the whole crew climbed up the rocky slopes of the Acropolis and walked around the Parthenon and all the other ruins. We were so lucky to be there in the days before mass tourism because only about a dozen other people were visiting the ruins on the day we were there. In the evening we ate in a small restaurant at the foot of the Acropolis, and when I went to the ladies' lavatory, I found it was extremely primitive – merely a hole in an earth floor. I was wearing a dress I'd designed myself that had a very tight skirt and around my waist there was a wide sash, pleated at the front like a man's cummerbund, and fastened at the back with long "tails" hanging down to the length of the skirt's hem. This was the worst lavatory I'd ever seen – including those in camps in game parks – but necessity drove me to use it. I straddled the "lavatory", wriggled my tight skirt *up* and my panties *down*, and half squatted over the disgusting hole in the ground. Suddenly I looked and realised – too late – that the "tails" of my sash were hanging into the well-used cess-pit! I managed to unfasten the sash and let it drop to the floor and I walked away, leaving it there. A little later, when half a dozen girls came out to perform in the cabaret, I realised that the primitive conditions of the ladies' lavatory shouldn't surprise me; this must have been a very impoverished part of the city of Athens because it was apparent that none of the dancing young women could afford any clothes!

When we acquired larger aircraft, the cold food that had been the standard aircraft meals until then, was replaced by hot food. At first, the hot food consisted of round plastic dishes or bowls that held a lunch or dinner main course, and these dishes were put on board in large insulated containers to keep the food hot. These round plastic dishes looked exactly like dog dishes… and that is the way we always referred to them. The food, having been kept hot for some hours in the insulated containers, did not taste very good and this is probably when airline food reached its lowest point and gained its reputation for being awful. The meals in "dog dishes" were only in use for about a year, and then the meals became much better when the main courses were put on board chilled, and the aircraft had ovens in which we cooked them.

No matter what improvements were made with the addition of ovens on board, the one thing that you cannot do on an aircraft is make a really good cup of tea. This is because water boils at a lower temperature when you are at several thousand feet above sea level. (Even pressurised aircraft are not pressurised to ground level, but only to between 5,000 and 8,000ft.) One day after we'd served lunch, the other air hostess was going round the cabin serving coffee. She came back to the galley to get the pots refilled and said, 'There is *such* a nice man down near the back. He just stopped me and asked if I could refill his cup because, he said, that was the best cup of tea he'd ever had on any flight.' I said to her, 'I hope you didn't spoil his pleasure by telling him it's coffee!'

Although the following story doesn't concern food and drink on board the aircraft, it is one that is worth telling. When we first flew to Accra, Ghana, in the late 1950s, the hotels were "minimalist" to say the least. The one we stayed in consisted of two long, two-storey, wooden buildings with corrugated iron roofs. One building was for males and one was for females. The first time I went to Ghana, I slept in the "female building" and got up next morning to walk over to the main building to have breakfast. As I stepped through the door to walk outside, I darted back inside thinking it was pouring with rain. But it wasn't rain; it was so humid that overnight moisture had collected on the roof, and was running down between the grooves in the corrugated roof, and draining off just like heavy rain. As time went by, modern buildings started to appear in Accra, including a large hotel.

One day when we arrived at this new hotel, the crew all dispersed to their rooms and when we met later for dinner, the captain said he had a funny story to tell us. He said that when he reached his room, he decided to take a bath. He ran a tub full of water, took off all his clothes, got into the bath and looked around for the soap. No soap! So he padded out with wet feet to the bedroom, and phoned down to reception and asked for some soap to be sent up to Room XXX. 'Just one moment, sir,'…. and after a few moments another voice answered, 'Room service.' 'Could I please have some soap in Room XXX?' 'Certainly, sir. What kind of soap would you like?' 'Oh, I don't mind… any sort of soap.' 'It will be there right away, sir.' The captain hung up and decided to leave the room door ajar, and get back into the bath to await the delivery of the soap.

In just a few minutes there was a knock on the bedroom door and he shouted, 'Come in.' He heard someone come into his bedroom and then a voice called out, 'Where would you like the soap, sir?' 'In here… in the bathroom, of course,' he answered. And then a waiter, carrying a tray, appeared through the bathroom door. There was a bowl on the tray and the waiter said, 'I have your soup here, sir.' Yes *soup*. A completely understandable misunderstanding!

Much as I usually enjoy curry, I never had one that I liked in either Bombay or Karachi so maybe they didn't "adjust the seasoning and flavourings" to cater to European palates. Of course, I was there half a century ago and everything is probably very different now.

In Kenya I had the best Pimm's I've ever drunk. In addition to putting the usual slices of lemon and cucumber and a sprig of mint into the drink, in Kenya they also add a "stick" of banana (made by cutting a piece of banana into four, longways), which makes a delicious difference to the flavour.

Of all the hotels I stayed in around the world while I was flying, some stand out in my memory. One in Rome had a swimming pool on the roof – swimming up there, with a view of the city, especially at night, was a delight. In Malta, we stayed in a hotel that had been converted from a monastery and although the rooms were very small, having been monks' cells, the hotel had a great deal of charm. It was built on a high point on the edge of the city of Medina, and the views were outstanding. From my bedroom (cell!) window I once watched the Red Arrows performing some of their flying aerobatics, and from my high vantage point I was actually looking down on them.

In Nairobi we usually stayed at the New Stanley Hotel, a good, modern hotel, but sometimes we stayed at The Norfolk, an older hotel which was still very much preferred by "the old Kenya hands". Having Sunday curry lunch at The Norfolk was a long-standing tradition in Kenya and, in contrast to my experiences of curries in Bombay and

Karachi, the ones served at The Norfolk were delicious. My recollections of this beautiful hotel are somewhat spoiled by the memory of a nightmare that I had on one occasion. Just as frightening as the nightmare itself is the fact that I found out later that I had dreamed about actual events that *had* happened there but of which I had no previous knowledge. Even more eerie is the fact that the radio officer, who had slept in that same room on our way south, had had what seemed to be an identical nightmare, in which he saw the same horrible events taking place. I didn't know what had happened to him, but when he heard about my frightening experience, he told me that after having a terrifying nightmare himself in that room, he did not want to sleep in it again. So when we returned to the hotel on the northbound leg of our journey, he had insisted that I should have the room that he'd been in on the way south. 'It's a much larger room than yours and it has a nicer bathroom,' he had said to me, so I simply thought it was a kind gesture and changed rooms.

Once when I was staying at a very well known hotel (which shall be nameless) on a Mediterranean island, I woke up after I'd been asleep for a short time feeling very "itchy". I turned on the light and looked and sure enough there were some large, itching bumps appearing on my legs and body. Looking more closely, I found that there were bed bugs crawling in my bed. Next morning I went to the reception desk and handed them a matchbox that was filled with bedbugs I'd killed.

The hotel we always stayed at in Benghazi opened a night club and a small casino within the hotel. I had always wanted to play roulette and one evening one of the men on the crew said that he'd take me into the casino and show me how to play. I changed some money into chips and we stood beside a table as he explained that I could bet my money (chip) on a single number, or a block of numbers, or a line of numbers. I've always liked the number 17, which is my birthday, and I immediately reached forward and put a chip on that number. My companion said, 'No, no... that's silly to put your money on just the one number. Although the odds are less, you should cover a block of numbers or...' Before he could finish, one of the croupiers called, 'Rien ne va plus,' and the wheel started to slow, and then the ball rattled into a slot. 'Dix-sept,' said the croupier. My number 17 had come up! This was obviously beginner's luck because I don't think I ever won again at roulette!

Chapter 10

The Rarity… the Unpleasant Passenger

Generally speaking, our passengers were thoroughly nice people, a pleasure to have aboard the aircraft. But inevitably, of course, there were some who were – to put it mildly – less nice. Occasionally there would be a passenger who was downright unpleasant and sometimes one who was deliberately rude.

One passenger who was known to be rude and "difficult" was a former Prime Minister of Great Britain. I won't say *which* former Prime Minister but I will say that in his public life, whenever he appeared either in person or on television, he was considered charming; a perfect gentleman. But as a passenger, he was known to be ill mannered to the point of rudeness. I suppose he could be described as having a "Dr Jekyll and Mr Hyde" personality, and whenever he was a passenger on one of our aircraft, the Mr Hyde side of his personality emerged. When he travelled with us, it was always on a special charter, and he would be travelling with Ministers and advisors, secretaries and assistants. Whenever an air hostess went along the cabin, asking if passengers would like a drink from the bar, she would obviously approach the former Prime Minister first to ask if she could get him a drink or anything else. He would never answer her directly. Presumably he considered her to be a serving wench, a minion, and although she was standing right next to him, he would speak only through one of his assistants. 'Tell her I'll have a whisky and soda, without ice.' 'Tell the girl I'll have another drink.' On one flight he was so consistently unpleasant that he reduced a very senior, very well experienced air hostess to tears. The only time I've ever known that to happen to any of our air hostesses.

By contrast, Sir Winston Churchill was courteous and pleasant. When a friend of mine had him on board as part of a government group travelling overseas, she made the usual pre-flight announcement giving the flying time to the destination, and the altitude at which they'd be flying. Then she added the standard, 'After the captain has turned out the "No Smoking" sign, you may smoke, but cigarettes only please, not pipes or cigars.' Shortly after take-off, one of Sir Winston's aides came to where she was working at the back of the aircraft and asked if Sir Winston may smoke a cigar. She was in a quandary. Regulations decreed that cigars should not be smoked in the cabin, but this *was* Sir Winston Churchill. She made a quick decision. 'I'll check with the other passengers and if nobody objects, then of course, he may smoke his cigar,' she said. Nobody said they would object to the smell of cigar smoke, so she was able to go along and tell Sir Winston that yes, he may smoke a cigar.

Another unpleasant person, someone none of us relished seeing coming aboard, was a man who is a well known television personality, and who was, at that time, the host of a chat show. Although, unlike the former Prime Minister, he *would* address the air hostess directly, he did so in a very nasty manner, and was always extremely rude. On one occasion, when he had been what could only be termed "verbally abusive" to the senior air hostess on board, she resigned on the spot! I have never known that to happen on any other occasion, with our airline or any other. However, resigning turned out to be the best thing she'd ever done; she immediately got another job with an immensely wealthy Greek shipping tycoon as an air hostess on the crew of his very luxurious personal aircraft, at almost double her previous salary. While working at that job, she met and married her husband and – just as in all the best stories – they have lived happily ever after.

Sometimes a passenger would try to "throw his weight about" and impress us, implying that he was a person of some importance. On one flight, a man grumbled and complained all the time, starting right after take-off from London. Nothing was right and everything was wrong. At one point he said to the air hostess who was in the cabin, 'I shall make a full report about this flight to your chairman. He's a very good friend of mine; we play golf together.' Without missing a beat, the air hostess turned her most brilliant smile on him and said, 'Oh how interesting… you play golf with my uncle!' (Of course, our chairman and that air hostess were no relation to each other! But it did stop Mr Complainer in his tracks!)

One day, a young man had been thoroughly obnoxious to all the cabin crew throughout the flight. They had all gritted their teeth and put up with his unpleasant behaviour for many hours (it was a very long flight) until, when dinner was being served, he looked at the tray placed in front of him, curled his lip, and drawled, 'Oh... is that what you call dinner? Don't I have a choice?' The air hostess who had served him was the daughter of an Earl, and thus a Lady in her own right, and she was not about to put up with any more of his nonsense. When he asked that question, she gave him a bright smile, looked him in the eye, and answered, 'Oh yes, sir, of course you have a choice. You can eat it... or you can leave it!'

A very famous actress, who was considered a great beauty in the 1950s, boarded a Viking flight that was going from London to Hamburg and then on to Berlin. As soon as she came through the door, she took off her full length mink coat, literally threw it at the air hostess, and snapped, 'Here, hang this up!' The Viking, being a very small aircraft, had no place to hang coats, so the mink coat was carefully laid on the floor behind the back row of seats. The air hostess thought that she would retrieve it and hand it to the actress before landing, so she'd never know that her precious coat had been lying on the floor and not hung up. Unfortunately, during the flight, the actress walked down to the back, saw her coat and screamed insults at the air hostess, ending with,

'You are the most unhelpful girl I've ever known!' and, taking careful aim, spat at her!

Air hostesses were supposed to be able to deal with any problems that may arise with passengers, and it was rare for any of the pilots to get involved with an unpleasant or complaining passenger, but it happened one day when a man had found fault with everything – his seat, the food, the drink, the service ... everything. When one of the air hostesses went up front to take some coffee to the crew, she told the captain about this man and his complaints that were all completely unreasonable and unjustified. The captain was a Liverpudlian who was always very good humoured, but he was not a man to put up with such absurd and unfounded complaints as this passenger was making. 'Tell me which seat he's in,' he said. A few minutes later, he strolled out of the cockpit, and started to walk through the cabin, having a word here and there with some of the passengers. When he reached the man with all the complaints he said, 'I understand you have not enjoyed your flight with us today, sir.' 'No, I have not,' was the answer, 'and I intend to complain in writing when I get back to England.' 'Well,' said the captain, 'may I make a suggestion?' 'Yes, of course,' said the man. 'If you will give me a name to write to, I'll address my letter directly to...' 'Oh no, you misunderstand me,' interrupted the captain. 'The suggestion I would like to make, sir, is that you never fly with us again. Please use another airline in future.'

I can remember only one other time when a pilot "had words" with a passenger. During a flight towards the Mediterranean, the captain made an announcement, 'If you look out on the right-hand side, there is an excellent view of the city of Paris.' This particular captain had had a distinguished and highly decorated wartime career with the RAF. Soon after making that announcement, he walked back through the cabin and was stopped by a young man. No doubt thinking he was being very clever, the young man asked, 'Are you the captain?' Then he went on, 'When you made that announcement, you shouldn't have said "right-hand side", you should have said "starboard".' The captain paused and looked at him for a long moment, then said, 'Ah yes... you are too young to know.... on bombing runs, when aiming for the target, we always talked about "the left" or "the right" hand side.'

One day a passenger told me that his daughter wanted to be an air hostess, and that she had applied to Hunting-Clan but had been turned down. 'I'd like to know,' he asked in a very aggressive manner, 'why *you* got a job with them, and she didn't. Why are *you* better than she is?' Obviously, I had no idea why she had been turned down and told him (truthfully) that we had hundreds of young women applying for just a handful of jobs, and therefore many of them had to be turned down. He went on to ask a lot of questions – what languages did I speak? What previous experience had I had that would be valuable to an airline? Had I worked for a hotel or in catering before joining the airline? Had I been a nurse? He continued in a very unpleasant way to make it clear that he couldn't see why *I* had been employed but his daughter hadn't. It would have given me a great deal of satisfaction to tell him that if his daughter had a personality like his, then I could see why she'd been rejected! But, of course, I applied my standard rule of "keep smiling and say nothing!"

One story is too good to omit even though it didn't happen to me or on British United Airways. On a flight to London on another major British airline, a woman who was travelling in First Class had been particularly obnoxious and had given the cabin crew a lot of trouble throughout the flight. As they neared London, she asked one of the air hostesses, 'What is the current situation in London for hiring domestic staff?' The air hostess replied, 'Oh London is really booming! I'm sure you won't have any problems obtaining a job madam.'

But I can't end on that sour note. I must repeat that, with very few exceptions, our passengers were delightful people. We certainly did not have to deal with the "air rage" that is heard about nowadays, when sometimes cabin crew have to put "restraints" on a passenger. Occasionally, some passengers seemed irritable if they were nervous, but almost always our passengers were thoroughly nice people. You will notice that this is a very short chapter. That in itself confirms that I have very few stories to tell about unpleasant passengers.

Chapter 11

Whoops!

After a chapter about unpleasant passengers, it is only fair that I should tell some stories that could be called "Whoops" … where the air hostess made some kind of a mistake.

A friend of mine was working on a flight that had been chartered to fly members of The Royal Ballet from London to Manchester. The famous prima ballerina Dame Margot Fonteyn was the most important member of the company on board. As it was a short flight, a meal would not be served but the passengers were to have "snacks". After serving drinks to all the passengers, my friend started to serve the "snacks" which were fairly substantial and needed a fork to eat them. To her horror she found that catering had not put any cutlery on board, and she hadn't checked before departure! The only thing to do was to be honest about it, and so she approached Dame Margot, explained the situation and apologised profusely. 'Don't worry,' said

Dame Margot, 'these people probably don't use cutlery at home anyhow.'

This same friend worked on a flight that had been chartered by Loel Guinness and his wife Gloria, along with Rosalind Russell and her husband Carl Brisson, to fly to Naples where they were going to board their yacht which was moored at Capri. The four of them were the only passengers on board and when they arrived in Naples, they invited the crew to go along to the yacht with them. Once aboard, they served what they described as "American martinis" and which my friend described as completely overpowering!

Although I was never invited aboard a private yacht, I did go to Naples several times but it was usually a fairly quick turn around or just overnight. At that time they had not yet put in a concrete runway there and they still had a metal mesh "runway" from wartime days. This made the most fearsome clatter when you landed – quite alarming the first time you landed there and didn't know what was making all the noise! Eventually I went to Naples and was scheduled to stay for two nights, with a day off in the middle. I very much wanted to see the island of Capri – it was the sort of place that one always thought of, or heard about, as being very 'glamorous'. It had featured in a popular song and after the end of WWII, the singer Gracie Fields had made her home there. My one day in Naples dawned grey and rain threatened but I was not deterred; I fully intended to get a boat over to Capri and look around. I went down to the reception desk of the hotel and asked about getting a taxi to wherever I had to go to get a boat to the island. The young Italian man on the reception desk gestured to the grey skies and said, 'Oh, madam, you should not go today. It is not nice to see Capri on a day like this. Capri without sunshine is… is… is…' Words failed him for just a moment and then he continued, '… is like seeing a beautiful woman and not kissing her.' (I'm tempted to ask 'Who else but an Italian man would think of that?')

'But I'm only here for one day… what other sights can I see?' I asked. By now the flight engineer had joined me at the reception desk and he, too, was wondering where to go and what to see. The young man said that there was a small active volcano called Solfatara at Pozzuoli, just five miles south of the city of Naples, and he thought we'd find that interesting. So we went to Pozzuoli, which we found was not only home to the Solfatara volcano, but was also the place where Sophia Loren had spent some of her childhood. The name Solfatara derives from the Italian word for sulphur, which was the overpowering smell all over the small town. Apparently, when Vesuvius is not active, Solfatara bubbles away, and narrow raised walkways had been constructed so that you could walk around the areas of grey, bubbling (smelly) lava. The heat given off by the volcanic mud reaches 160 degrees Centigrade and even though I was on the walkways around the edges of the eruption, the soles of my shoes were scorched. So… it wasn't Capri, but walking around an active volcano (albeit a small one) was something I'd never done before and I've never done it since.

Something one of the air hostesses did (or rather didn't do) was even worse than not checking that the cutlery was on board – she didn't check that meals were on board! She boarded the aircraft for a flight that was going non-stop from Bathurst in The Gambia, West Africa, to London. She checked that everything was in order in the cabin and the lavatories, and she checked that the galley had been cleaned, and that the several water containers had been filled with fresh water. The canisters containing meals were all in place... but the only thing she didn't do was open any of the meal canisters. Had she done so, she would have found that instead of being full of meals ready for her to serve, they contained trays with the remains of a meal that had already been served on the incoming flight! These canisters should have been taken out of the galley and put in the hold, and the canisters that contained the meals for the Bathurst to London flight should have been brought up from the hold and loaded in the galley. It was only after they were airborne that she discovered that instead of trays full of fresh meals, all she had were trays full of leftovers! How do you get around a problem like this? I think she showed great initiative; she got the other hostess to help her and they put together "snack meals" made up from whatever they could scavenge from the leftovers on the used dinner trays! They served these "snacks" on small trays with copious quantities of tea and coffee. As she puts it, 'Nobody complained... but equally, nobody asked for more.'

I once did something similar when the main course of a meal suddenly slipped out of my hand and landed upside down on the galley floor. Usually, in case of just such accidents, we carried a couple of extra meals but on this particular flight we had exactly the right number of meals for the passengers on board. I carefully picked up everything from the floor, re-arranged it on the tray, and sent the meal out – without anybody being any the wiser!

In the winter there were package holidays to ski resorts, and one of the advertised features was that "Your holiday starts as soon as you board your aircraft, when you will be served a hot toddy." The hot toddies were free, part of the all-inclusive price of the holiday, and usually three bottles of brandy were put in the bar for us to use for these drinks. On one flight, I didn't check the bar for the "free bottles" and after we were airborne when I started to make the hot toddies, I found that there was only one bottle of brandy! How could I stretch this to make hot toddies for each of the 64 passengers? Someone on the crew had the bright idea that I should put the mix of lemon, sugar and hot water into glasses, and then simply wipe brandy generously around the rim of the glass. 'They will *smell* the brandy, and their lips will touch it, and they will never know there isn't a slug of brandy in the mix,' he said. And he was right!

Another "Whoops" happened when the crew assembled in Operations before a flight and the junior air hostess who would be working in the cabin on my flight proudly showed me the artificial nails she had applied. They certainly looked very glamorous; they were long, and a lovely cherry red. We were about to set off on a lengthy trip, and I asked her, 'How long will they stay on?' 'Oh, the girl in the shop where I bought them said they will stay on for ages…' she said airily. And they did indeed stay on for a couple of days until, after clearing away the dinner trays, she was offering a cheese tray to passengers. She asked each passenger to cut off pieces of whichever cheese they wanted, and then help themselves to the spring onions, and halved small tomatoes that we had put on the tray by way of decoration. One man cut off a piece of cheese. 'Oh good… lovely Stilton,' he said. 'Oh and a radish… I'll take that.' Except it wasn't a radish. It was a cherry-red artificial thumbnail that had come off and landed on the cheese tray!

That story went around the whole airline very quickly, and after hearing it, a friend of mine said that she'd been contemplating wearing false eyelashes but now she'd decided not to. 'Just think how awful it would be if one of my false lashes fell off into a passenger's cup of coffee!'

I remember a couple of examples of not so much a "Whoops!" as quick thinking that saved the situation.

One day a passenger asked the air hostess for 'A pink gin, please.' The passenger was a very well known, very wealthy man, who also happened to be a major shareholder in the airline. The air hostess was completely nonplussed and admits that she had no idea just what a "pink gin" was… pink champagne, yes, she'd heard of that, but a drink called "a pink gin"? She looked him straight in the eye and said, 'Oh, sir, a pink gin is such an individual drink… so much a matter of personal taste… how do you like yours made?' Almost exactly a year later, he was again a passenger on one of her flights. As she went round taking orders for drinks she turned to him and asked, 'Mr X, would you like your usual pink gin?' He was so impressed that he wrote to the Chief Air Hostess, saying that this girl was a credit to the airline!

One of our aircraft was chartered to fly out to Spain and bring home a winning rugby team, plus their substitutes, and coaching staff. When these passengers boarded it was immediately obvious to the air hostess that they had been celebrating their victory, not wisely but too well! After take-off, they all had another drink or two and became increasingly noisy and boisterous. But they were all happy drunks and didn't present any problems until they started to make rather too many advances to the air hostess. Every time she climbed over the main spar (the "two steps up, and two steps down") there were raucous catcalls and whistles, and then one or two of them made a grab at her, asking for a kiss. She decided that the time had come to close the bar, and serve a meal. While she was serving the meal, she realised that they were continuing to drink because they'd opened up the duty-free bottles that they'd purchased in Spain and brought on board. She had an inspired thought, and turned up the heating on the aircraft. The combination of all the booze plus the warmth had the desired effect... the passengers were soon asleep. Sleeping soundly, if not quietly! But snores she could cope with and she'd de-fused a situation that was rapidly getting out of hand.

Chapter 12

Accidents *Can* Happen

One word that is never mentioned by an airline, or any of its staff, is "accident". And certainly not the word "crash". Maybe, back in the 1950s, this was a very early example of "spin". Airlines would only ever refer to an "incident" or a "problem" or at most an "emergency". However, whether they are mentioned or not, accidents *do* happen. Mercifully, they happen only rarely.

Soon after I started flying – in fact, it was only my sixth flight – we were chartered by Aquila Airways, an airline that doesn't exist now. Aquila was an airline that operated flying boats from Southampton to several destinations in Europe, including the Italian Riviera, and also to Las Palmas and Madeira. Aquila had had an accident (fortunately non fatal) with one of their flying boats at Santa Margherita, and as they were therefore short of an aircraft until that one was repaired, they chartered Hunting-Clan to carry their passengers on some flights. I was working on an Aquila chartered flight to Geneva and as well as the passengers, an Aquila air hostess called Muriel Hanning-Lee was on board. She had been flying for some years, and I'd only been flying for a matter of weeks, and as they were really "her" passengers, obviously I let her decide on timing of drinks and meal service. We got along very well and I was thrilled to hear that she'd written a book that was to be published early the next year, 1958. I promised her that when the book came out, I would buy a copy. I did, and I still have it. Unfortunately, Muriel did not live to see her book published. On 15th November 1957, she was the air hostess on board an Aquila Airways flying boat that took off from Southampton bound for Las Palmas. The aircraft crashed on the Isle of Wight, killing many of those on board, including Muriel.

In August 1958, I was flying in a Viscount on a northbound leg of our East African service. We flew from Entebbe to Khartoum, then Wadi Halfa, and when we reached Benghazi we disembarked, and another crew took the flight on to London. We had landed in the early hours of the morning and when we got up next day, we heard that a Central African Airways Viscount that was flying almost the same route as we had flown, and which should have landed at Benghazi about 15 minutes behind us, had crashed just short of the runway. Thirty-six people had lost their lives, and the survivors had been taken to the British military hospital just outside Benghazi. At that time, the British military presence in that area was in the process of being wound down and although the hospital was technically still open, unfortunately there were only two doctors and two or three nurses still working there. My "number two" hostess had been a nurse and we talked about what had happened, and decided to contact the hospital and ask if they needed any blood donated. We were told that they didn't need blood but they did need help, and we were asked if we would go out to the hospital and assist. As we were scheduled to have three days off, obviously we said yes, and a car was sent to take us to the hospital. On the way, I must admit I had some qualms as I wondered just what sights would confront us when we reached the hospital. We knew that all the survivors were suffering from burns and we knew that some were not expected to survive. As the other air hostess was a qualified nurse, she went off with one of the doctors to help with some of the most severely injured patients, and I was sent to a room where two injured children lay in cots. Neither of the children had yet been identified. One was a boy aged about eight months, with terrible burns and head injuries; the other was a little girl of three or four who had a broken arm and some burns that were not severe.

The baby boy was on a drip and unconscious, but the little girl was awake, alert and hungry. I gave her whatever food she would eat and kept her drinking plenty of fluids, and while doing that, I asked her, 'What's your name?' She got all giggly and wouldn't tell me her name. 'You must guess,' she said. Not useful or helpful! So I changed the subject and started to talk to her about her home and family, so that I could try to establish some facts that might help in identifying her. None of the survivors had had a little girl travelling with them, and a copy of the passenger list had not yet arrived, so we were really groping in the dark. I asked her if she had a dog or a cat, and when she said yes, she had a dog, I asked its name. She told me the dog's name, and then, trying to ascertain her age, I asked if she'd had a party for her birthday? She said, 'Yes,' and told me that she was four. 'What name does your mummy call your daddy, and what name does your daddy call your mummy?' I asked – anything to try to get some pieces of information.

The next day, when I went to the hospital, I asked her, 'Do you remember my name from yesterday?' She did. So I said, 'Well *you* know *my* name… don't you think it would be fair to tell me *your* name?' Success! 'My name is Elizabeth*,' she said. Very soon after we'd established her name, there was a contact from her grandparents in England. We found out that Elizabeth had been flying to London with her mother to visit the grandparents, and her father had stayed behind in Rhodesia and had planned to fly to London himself a week or so later.

Elizabeth's condition was stable, and it was decided to fly her to London for treatment at Great Ormond Street Hospital for Sick Children. When I arrived back in England, I went to visit her there and met her father. Although nobody had recognised her, Elizabeth was a little girl who had already been in the news, when she had been at the centre of sensational newspaper stories that had hit the headlines a year or two earlier. Her mother, who was travelling with her and had been killed in the crash, was actually her adoptive mother.

(*Elizabeth is not her real name; I have changed her name because she is probably still alive, a woman who is now in her mid-50s.)

My next, and last, "close encounter" with a crash came later that same year. In December 1958, Hunting-Clan had its only major accident when one of our Viscounts crashed in Surrey. The aircraft, registration G-ANRR, was one I had worked on only a few weeks before. It had had routine maintenance work carried out and as is the normal practice following such work, the aircraft was taken up for a test flight before being put back into passenger service. The Viscount took off from London Airport, and just 12 minutes later, the captain radioed that the aircraft was out of control. Eight minutes after that, it crashed and burst into flames, killing all the crew of six who were on board. The captain was our Chief Pilot – the one who had sent for me and asked if I felt able to take out a flight on my own.

The aircraft had been scheduled to leave on a regular flight from London to Nairobi later that same day. I was on the crew that was waiting in Benghazi to board that aircraft and fly south. As usual before a late night take-off, we had gone out to eat dinner (the cooking in the bedrooms having been stopped some time before) and when we returned to the hotel we were greeted by the hotel manager in tears, saying, 'Oh captain, oh captain, such awful news… your aircraft…'

Chapter 13

Go East, Young Woman!

Late in 1961, British United Airways was awarded a contract by the Ministry of Defence to carry troops and their families to the Far East. We would be carrying these passengers to Hong Kong and to Singapore, and this gave me the opportunity to see that part of the world for the first time. When we first operated these "trooping flights", we would "slip" in either Bombay or Karachi, spending just two or three days there and we would then work the next flight to the Far East, but later a whole crew was posted to Bombay for a month at a time. This crew then worked as a shuttle crew, taking flights on from Bombay to and from Hong Kong, and to and from Singapore. The crew that had worked from England stayed in Bombay and then worked the homeward bound Bombay-London sector.

As Bombay had strict laws about the sale of alcohol at that time, when we spent a month there as the shuttle crew we were each issued with a "drinking permit". This meant that, as long as we showed the permit, we were allowed to buy a drink – spirits, wine or beer – when having a meal in a restaurant or in the hotel. The permits were all printed in the local script so we couldn't read what was written on them but I was told that each of us was registered as an alcoholic! Whether that was true or not, I never found out.

While I was in Bombay for a month as part of the shuttle crew, we heard about an Indian fortune-teller who was said to be very clever at seeing into the future, and one day several crew members went to visit her. For some reason – I can't remember why – I didn't go, and when they came back and I heard what she'd told each of them about their future life, I was glad that I had not gone because all her predictions seemed to be doom and gloom. I remember her dismal prophecies for one of the air hostesses. She told her that she would marry soon (she was already engaged, so it wasn't too difficult for anybody to make that forecast, just by looking at her left hand!) but that she would be 'surrounded by divorce and courts of law.' That didn't seem to indicate a happy married life for her, but as it happened, this girl married (and is still married to) a lawyer who built up a very successful practice, specialising in divorce law!

Soldiers travelling with their wives and children were referred to by the Ministry of Defence as "married families". I'm not sure if it was the MoD or the military authorities who designated three types of "married families": Officers and their ladies; non-commissioned officers and their wives; other ranks and their women.

Soon after we'd won this contract, one of the royal dukes was posted to Hong Kong. His wife and children were to fly out to join him there, and the newspapers carried stories saying that "the Duchess" would travel just like any other army officer's wife and no special provisions would be made on account of her royal status. These newspaper stories were absolutely true; she and her children travelled on our aircraft in exactly the same seats and section of the cabin as the other officers' wives and families.

One of the conditions of this contract was that we would serve five main meals and two sub-meals in every 24-hour period. We could never quite work out what the five main meals were to be. Obviously breakfast is one main meal; mid-morning coffee and biscuits and some kind of snack was a sub-meal; lunch would be a main meal; tea in the afternoon with sandwiches and cake would be the second sub-meal; dinner would be the next main meal; and then later we would serve supper which was another main meal. But breakfast, lunch, dinner and supper only add up to four main meals. How and when were we to serve the fifth main meal? Somehow, we always managed to fit it in, though many of the passengers said they would prefer to be left to sleep rather than be woken up to be given their fifth main meal!

On the "trooping flights" there were always a lot of children and small babies. To accommodate babies, we had an ingenious piece of equipment called a "Skycot". These were firm plastic gondola shapes with large hooks on each end. There were overhead racks for small pieces of baggage and the Skycots hooked over the edge of the racks. Inside the Skycot was a mattress and a blanket, and babies usually slept very well in them. The slight movement of the aircraft and the low drone of the engines seemed to help them sleep. Sometimes, of course, like all babies the world over, they would wake up and cry, and I can assure you that it is a myth that a mother recognises her own baby's cry. I have seen too many women sound asleep beneath their baby in its Skycot, and the mother would continue to sleep right through the yells that were waking up everybody else!

Sometimes mothers would come aboard with several bottles of the baby's food ready mixed and when the baby was due for a feed, the mother would hand us the bottle and ask us to heat it slightly. We really appreciated those well-prepared mothers, because many others came aboard with their tins of powdered baby food, which they would hand to us with instructions for mixing it to their own specifications. 'Three scoops of X brand baby food and 6oz of water, no sugar'; 'Four scoops of Y brand baby food and 8oz of water, with a teaspoon of sugar'; 'Three scoops of the Z brand baby food, and 7oz of water, and a spoon of malt' and so on. We'd end up with half a dozen or more different brands of baby food lined up on the counter top in the galley, and scribbled notes of what to add and how much to give to the different infants. At first I used to worry a great deal about getting "the mix" right, and being sure that I'd used the brand that the baby was used to having. But as time went on and I worked more and more "trooping flights", each with their many babies, I will confess that I took the easy way out. I simply used a scoop from each of the tins of baby food, added water to make it up to the quantity the mother had specified, and then I always added a little sugar. I thought that the babies who were used to having sugar would scream with rage and refuse to suck if they didn't have a nice sweet mixture, and the ones who didn't normally get sugar in their bottle would be delighted with this delicious new taste. My philosophy must have been right, because it always seemed to work – lots of happy babies all sucking contentedly!

Because there were always so many young babies on these "trooping flights" we carried a supply of nappies in the hold. These were for use in case we were delayed anywhere along the route. On one flight, less than an hour after take-off, a mother asked if we had any nappies and I assured her that we had plenty in the hold for use if we were delayed. She said that she needed one now and I had to repeat that I couldn't get to them because they were in the hold and, in any case, they were only for use if we were delayed. She was not at all pleased when I told her this and said, 'Well, I need one *now*. I put a clean nappy on him at London Airport. I didn't know it was going to take so long to get to Hong Kong!'

On the way to Hong Kong and Singapore we had to land in either Bombay (now Mumbai) or Karachi to refuel. During refuelling, all the passengers had to disembark and, even though they were confined to the airport and were only in transit for the time it took to refuel, all the troops had to travel in civilian clothes because the authorities in both Pakistan and India would not allow "military personnel" to pass through their territory, even when merely in transit.

For all of the air hostesses the great pleasure of the airline winning this "trooping contract" was that it took us to Hong Kong and Singapore, both well known as wonderful places to shop for almost anything.

We usually had a couple of days off in Singapore, and about 36 hours turn around in Hong Kong. No matter how tired we were when we arrived, the thought of all the things we could buy at extremely low prices soon galvanized us into action!

In Singapore, I bought a Noritake dinner and tea service with 12 complete place settings, which cost only about £10 and when I brought it back to England, Customs charged me ten shillings' duty on it. I still have it.

In Hong Kong we could buy beautiful clothing and fabulous jewellery at bargain basement prices. The Hong Kong tailors are famous for being able to take measurements and make up a man's suit, in the cloth of his choice, in just a couple of days and they would also make women's clothing. In both Bombay and Hong Kong, we would go to local shops, taking a sketch of a dress we wanted made, and choose the fabric (always pure silk). They would take our measurements and the garment would be completed and delivered to our hotel within a day or two. Somehow, without ever having a fitting or trying on the garment, it would always be perfect. And in both Bombay and Hong Kong a pure silk dress, made to our own sketched design, cost no more than two or three pounds!

Whatever we bought abroad had to be declared to Customs on our return to England and although we came through "Crew Customs" we were always treated in exactly the same way as any other returning travellers who were bringing goods into the country.

Chapter 14

That was Then; This is Now...

Looking back over all the intervening years since I was an air hostess (how can it possibly be almost half a century since I left the airline?) I am amazed by many things.

Firstly, when I remember things that some "elderly passengers" told me, I realise that the "elderly passenger" was probably younger then than I am now! And if I add together the years covered by the passenger's memories of events many years before, and my re-telling the story today, the "joint memories" span almost 100 years. For example, the man who told me, in 1958, about flying over enemy lines in the First World War (and feeling quite safe from enemy gunfire because they were flying at 30mph) was recalling events that had happened some 41 years earlier. And now, as I tell his story over 50 years after he told it to me, it is more than 90 years since he made those reconnaissance flights.

In the same way, the memories of the woman who had, as a young girl, danced at embassy balls in St Petersburg and my retelling her stories now, spans almost 100 years. She was telling me about a place and a time that sounded so glamorous and did not exist any more.

If I am a passenger on a flight nowadays, I can truthfully say that I do not envy the cabin crew. At the time I was flying, we had so much more time on board to get to know our passengers, and we had so much more time off-duty in various parts of the world. And, of course, we had what I consider a far better ratio of men to women on the crew! Now, not only are there often as many as ten female cabin crew members, but of the two pilots on board, one may well be a woman! I suppose, in fact, *both* pilots could be women! (A female pilot was even numbered among British Airways Concorde crews.) A couple of the "girls" who were air hostesses with me have daughters who, in their turn, became cabin crew. They always say that their daughters thoroughly enjoy their jobs but then we look at each other and say, 'But it's not like it was in the good old days. We had the *best* time.'

I deplore the attitudes of the 1950s and 1960s that said that a young woman might be considered "past it" by her 30th birthday, and gave the airline the right to demand her resignation when she reached that age. Nowadays, of course, there are laws barring discrimination on the grounds of age, and there are quite a few "air hostesses" who are still flying even in their 50s. Many of them do an excellent job and obviously care about their passengers and their comfort.

We observed the airline's rules exactly; if we didn't, we would be called in by the Chief Hostess and reprimanded for whatever it was that we were doing wrong. It could be something as trivial as wearing black gloves after a certain date in the spring, when we should have started wearing white gloves. Or 'Your hair is getting long… either get it cut, or put it up' was probably the most frequently heard reprimand. We were not allowed simply to tie our hair back, it had to be "put up" as soon as it got to collar length.

Although, as with any job, we sometimes got bored, we would always ask each other 'But what else could I *do*? What else would be as interesting as *this*?' and we always came back to the thought that if we left the airline, we would be changing not only our job, but also our lifestyle. A couple of our air hostesses did leave Hunting-Clan and joined Pan American Airways (an airline that no longer exists) where they earned quite a lot more money, and worked considerably fewer hours – the Americans had regulations governing the hours per month that cabin crew could work.

I've already talked briefly about what went on when crews were away from home on lengthy trips. Even now, when we get together at the reunions, some of the men who were the most notorious womanisers still think they have irresistible charms, and although they are now in their late 70s to mid-80s, they still flirt outrageously. (I realise I'm being sexist when I talk only about men who were womanisers, so I must admit that there were a few girls who were not noted for the strength of their knicker elastic!) Some of those "most notorious" men were married with children and not only having flings while they were away down the route but were, in a few cases, continuing the affairs back in England. One man who did this was actually having affairs with two air hostesses at the same time, and furthermore, the two girls had been friends for several years! Girlfriend A did not know that he had started a second affair with her friend whom I will call Girlfriend B, although of course, Girlfriend B knew of his longstanding affair with Girlfriend A. At one point, Girlfriend A met me for lunch and was very upset because, she said, 'He will never stay all night with me now. He says he has to go home because his wife is getting suspicious and doesn't believe that he always spends the night at his club in London.' She did not find out for months that when he would not spend the night with her, he was not going home to his wife as he claimed, but was leaving her and spending the night with Girlfriend B!

I had the misfortune (or was stupid enough?) to get engaged to the first officer who was known as the "Airline Romeo" – that same one who had taken me out to dinner in Valletta on my first overnight stop-over as a crew member. (He would probably be one of the men who still tries to flirt, if he came to one of the reunions.) Because we were both flying all the time, we would pass each other down the route, or just miss each other in England, for several weeks at a time. One day, when he had just arrived back in England from a lengthy trip, he telephoned and asked me to meet him at a bar near Heathrow Airport. When I arrived, he was already there and was chatting to an attractive young woman. He introduced us, and then went to get a drink for me. I noticed that she, too, was wearing an engagement ring and I thought that perhaps she was engaged to someone who was also with the airline. So I said, 'I see you are engaged. When do you plan to get married? And is your fiancé anything to do with airlines?' She looked quite surprised and said, 'Oh, didn't you know… I'm engaged to X.' "X" was just now coming back to the table, carrying the drink I'd asked for. I thought I hadn't heard her correctly, and asked, 'What? You are engaged to…?' I cannot imagine what was in his mind when he deliberately brought us together like this. Whatever he might have expected, I don't think it ever crossed his mind that his two "fiancées" would be so angry at being treated in this cavalier way, that we became quite good friends, and promptly "ganged up" on him! He left Hunting-Clan very soon after this incident and joined another airline. I kept the rather pretty antique ruby and diamond engagement ring. Wouldn't you, in the circumstances?

And finally…..

On 29th June, 1962, I was the senior air hostess on board a British United Airways Britannia aircraft that flew in from Freetown, Sierra Leone, and landed at Gatwick Airport. I said goodbye to the passengers as they disembarked, picked up my handbag, walked down the steps, and made my way to Crew Customs. The flight to and from Freetown had taken exactly nine hours each way, and in total I'd been on duty for 23 hours and 5 minutes. After I'd been cleared by

Customs, I went home and took off my uniform for the last time.

Despite the low pay, the long hours, the occasional bad tempered passenger, and a scare or two, for five years, one month and nine days, I'd had the time of my life!

The End